IBIZA AND FORMENTERA

SUE BRYANT

★★★ Highly recommended
★★ Recommended
★ See if you can

This edition is published by Connaught
an imprint of New Holland Publishers Ltd
London • Cape Town • Sydney • Auckland
First published in MCMXCVIII
10 9 8 7 6 5 4 3 2 1

website: www.newhollandpublishers.com

Garfield House, 86 Edgware Road
London W2 2EA, United Kingdom

80 McKenzie Street, Cape Town 8001,
South Africa

14 Aquatic Drive, Frenchs Forest, NSW 2086,
Australia

218 Lake Road, Northcote, Auckland,
New Zealand

ISBN 1 84537 145 3

Publishing Manager (UK): Simon Pooley
Publishing Manager (SA): Thea Grobbelaar
DTP Cartographic Manager: Genené Hart
Editors: Melany McCallum, Mary Duncan, Anouska Good, Pete Duncan
Design and DTP: Nicole Engeler, Sonia Cupido, Simon Lewis
Picture Researcher: Rowena Curtis
Cartographers: Marisa Galloway, John Hall
Compiler: Elaine Fick
Reproduction by Hirt & Carter (Pty] Ltd
Printed and bound by Times Offset (M) Sdn. Bhd., Malaysia.

Photographic Credits:
Alvey & Towers, 28; **Axiom/Steve Benbow**, 19, 63; **Chris Fairclough Colour Library**, 22 (bottom), 60, 72; **Footprints/Nick Hanna**, cover (bottom right), 21, 40, 43 (top), 58, 116; **Jeroen Snijders;** cover (top right), 7, 10, 11, 13 (top and bottom), 14, 17, 22 (top), 24, 25, 26, 27, 34, 41, 45 (top), 56, 57 (bottom), 62, 69, 70, 73, 74, 76, 85 (top), 89, 90, 92, 99 (top and bottom), 100, 101, 111, 114, 118 (top); **Jon Davison**, 15, 36, 43 (bottom), 48, 59, 104 (top), 113 (bottom), 115, 119; **Life File/Emma Lee**, 23, 46 (top), 57 (top), 75, 79, 84, 87, 91; **Peter Ryan**, 113 (top); **Photobank/Adrian Baker**, 4, 8, 39, 46 (bottom), 47, 55 (top and bottom), 66, 78, 93 (bottom), 103, 104 (bottom), 105, 117; **Photobank/Peter Baker**, 1, 16, 29, 71, 86, 108; **Spanish National Tourist Office**, cover (top left), 18, 37, 77; **Travel Ink/ Angela Hampton**, cover (bottom left), 6, 9 (top and bottom), 20, 30, 33, 35, 44, 45 (bottom), 49, 52, 61, 82, 88, 93 (top), 96, 102, 112, 118 (bottom).

Cover Photographs:
Top left: *Traditional dancers entertain a crowd at the village of Sant Miquel.*
Top right: *The fortifications of Dalt Villa.*
Bottom left: *Bathers and luxury yachts share the intimacy of Cala Vedella on the south coast.*
Bottom right: *Diners at a restaurant in Eivissa enjoy the summer atmosphere.*

Title Page: *A view of the Puerto La Savina harbour.*

CONTENTS

1 Introducing Ibiza and Formentera

Dazzlingly white in the Mediterranean sun, the tiny islands of Ibiza and Formentera deserve every bit of their reputation as a hedonist's dream. Hidden coves of aquamarine water overlooked by cliffs cloaked in bottle-green pines contrast with the neon lights of the most sophisticated nightlife in the Mediterranean. Sleepy villages bright with the islands' characteristic whitewash seem a million miles from the non stop entertainment of **Sant Antoni** or the cocktail bars and impromptu fashion shows of **Eivissa**, the capital and summer haunt of Europe's beautiful and outrageous society.

Both islands have been subject to waves of conquerors, all of whom have left their mark on the architecture, the food and the culture. One survival is the name given to the islands by early Greek traders – the **Pitiusas**, or 'pine islands' – which is a good description of Ibiza's hilly and wooded interior. As a result of the island's topography developers have mostly restricted their building to the coast where big, brash, high-rise resorts like Sant Antoni and **Platja d'en Bossa** serve a young, fun-loving market. In contrast, Eivissa's magnificent **Dalt Vila**, the walled medieval city, rests solidly on its hill, guarding the entrance to the harbour.

Across a now submerged natural causeway lies the sleepy island of **Formentera**, a complete contrast to its lively neighbour. Thick pine forests at the island's far end slope down to chequered farmland, dotted with tiny hamlets. Daytrippers exploring the country lanes by bicycle have little trouble finding peace and solitude here.

Top Attractions

*** **Dalt Vila:** Eivissa's fortified medieval town.
*** **Es Canar:** site of the weekly hippie market.
*** **Formentera:** wide-open spaces and breathtaking turquoise sea.
** **Dazzling nightlife:** the 'Ibiza scene' and Europe's most famous clubs.
** **Ses Salines:** shimmering salt pans.
* **Balafi:** Ibiza's only remaining Arabic village.
* **Remote coves and beaches:** accessible by walking or boat.

Opposite: *Houses soak up the warm Mediterranean sun in Eivissa's Dalt Vila.*

THE LAND

Red sandstone, limestone and basaltic rock make up the islands of Ibiza and Formentera, both of which have dramatic red cliffs, ancient cave formations and coastlines with rocky coves and long stretches of sand.

Ibiza is the most southerly of the Balearic islands, covering 572km² (221 sq miles). The island's highest peak, **Sa Talaiassa**, is 475m high (1558ft) but Ibiza is fairly hilly throughout. Its northern range, **Els Amunts**, is the most remote area with little tourist development around the coast. The centre is slightly flatter and the south more undulating. Much of the island is cultivated with orchards and ploughed fields, and the contrast of greenery or a stark white village against the open red soil is stunning.

Tiny islets are scattered all around the coast, most uninhabited apart from a solitary lighthouse. Formentera, 17.6km (11 miles) to the southeast, is shaped like a lop-sided dumbbell. Gentle hills at one end are joined to much steeper cliffs at the far side, rising 192m (630ft) above sea level, by a flat central strip just 1km (⅔ mile) wide in places. The natural causeway that once linked the two islands now forms a dangerous chain of jagged rocks requiring careful navigation.

FACT FILE

Size of Ibiza: 572km² (221 sq miles)
Size of Formentera: 82km² (32 sq miles)
Population of Ibiza: 73,300
Population of Formentera: 5000
Total number of restaurants: 632
Total number of nightclubs: 85
European Union 'Blue Flag' beaches: 18
Visitors per year: approx. two million
Sources of income: tourism and the 60,000 tons of salt exported annually to the Spanish mainland.

Rivers

Ibiza has the only river in the Balearics, the Santa Eulària, which rises in the hills near **Sant Mateu** and flows into the sea just outside a town that shares the same name as the river. The word 'flows' must be used loosely: the river is dry for much of the year and even after a rainy period is little more than a trickle. Water on both islands comes from artesian wells as there are no desalination plants.

Saltpans

Both Ibiza and Formentera have extracted and exported salt for centuries. In Ibiza, the saltpans are in the far south near the airport, forming a surreal environment of still, shimmering pools divided by narrow walls and overlooked by a glittering white mountain of salt.

Formentera's saltpans are in the northeast and like those of Ibiza, attract a wide variety of seabirds.

Beaches

The majority of Ibiza's 56 beaches are tiny, secluded coves accessible only by dirt track or boat. Sand beaches that are developed include **Platja d'en Bossa**, **Cala Llonga**, **Es Canar**, **Cala Sant Vicent** and **Platja de Sant Miquel** – all of which are very busy in July and August. Strangely, the longest stretches of sand in the south – the beaches of **Ses Salines** and **Es Cavallet** – are some of the least developed or crowded. Es Cavallet is a gay nudist beach and naturism is also practised at one end of Ses Salines. At both, the sea floor slopes gently away and the beaches are backed by scrub and pine-covered dunes. Formentera's long sandy strip, **Platja de Migjorn**, is absolutely stunning and always has space for sunbathers, while the water at the rocky cove of Es Caló is an astonishing shade of turquoise that rivals anything seen in the Caribbean.

Creatures of the Past

Sadly, several beautiful animals no longer roam the islands of Ibiza and Formentera. The **marten**, a small, weasel-like rodent, is extinct and the **genet**, a striking and distant relative of the domestic cat, is almost extinct. **Monk seals** used to bask on the rocks around the coast and rear their young in the shallow waters of the Balearics, and some elderly fishermen still speak of the colonies of **turtle** that used to spawn on the islands' sandy beaches. **Dolphins** are very occasionally spotted off the cliffs of La Mola on Formentera, but increasingly seldom.

Opposite: *A lone carob tree stands out against a field of red soil, characteristic of Ibiza's landscape.*
Below: *Formentera is fringed by waters of various breathtaking shades of blue.*

Climate

Ibiza and Formentera enjoy a typically Mediterranean climate; hot and dry in summer, cooler and occasionally wet in winter. Because winters are slightly cooler than on the mainland or in the other Balearic islands, the tourist season runs only from May to October; outside these months everything closes down and peace reigns.

The first charter flights arrive in May when the weather is usually clear but sometimes rainy and windy. Nights can turn chilly at any time outside July and August and spring temperatures average 17°C (63°F) in May. The sea only warms up in June and averages between 21°C (70°F) and 26°C (79°F) until October. Rain falls mainly in the cooler months with February, April and October being the wettest.

During the busy summer months, daily highs can reach 35°C (95°F) and most people simply sprawl on the beach. Cooling sea breezes make a day by the water slightly more tolerable.

Formentera enjoys the same temperatures as Ibiza although it can get very windy, particularly along the flat central stretch and the vast, sandy beach of the Migjorn, a popular haunt for windsurfers. Because of these breezes, Formentera is cool enough for cycling and hiking at any time of year. In Ibiza, however, hikers should stick to the coastal paths during summer. On more unpredictable days it is not uncommon for Formentera to be drenched in sunshine and Ibiza cloaked in cloud, or vice versa.

Snow, natural disasters and earthquakes are virtually unheard of on both islands.

Climate

Ibiza enjoys a near-perfect climate, with some 300 days of sunshine a year and a blissful 10 hours daily in summer. Summer days are hot, with averages of 25°C (77°F) and 26°C (79°F) in July and August. Daily highs peak at up to 35°C (95°F). Winters, however, are cooler than elsewhere in the Balearics, with daily average highs of 12°C (54°F) in January and February.

People swim in the sea off both islands from May to November, although the water temperature only reaches a comfortable 21°C (71°F) in June; sea swimming in May is for the hardy.

IBIZA & FORMENTERA	J	F	M	A	M	J	J	A	S	O	N	D
AVERAGE TEMP. °F	54	53	56	59	63	71	77	79	72	68	61	56
AVERAGE TEMP. °C	12	12	13	15	17	22	25	26	22	20	16	13
Hours of Sun Daily	4	4	6	8	6	11	11	12	8	6	5	4
RAINFALL in	1.6	2.4	1.4	1.2	0.6	0.2	0.3	0	0.3	1.5	1.1	0.7
RAINFALL mm	39	51	34	32	17	6	8	0	8	38	28	17
Days of Rainfall	5	14	10	15	3	2	4	0	2	12	6	3

Ca Eivissenc

Ibiza's own breed of dog, the Ca Eivissenc, looks like a cross between a greyhound and a whippet, with large ears and a pointed face. It originates from Egypt, where images have been found in bas-relief on tombs 4000 years old. This graceful but not particularly intelligent dog is prized for its hunting skills. It has an acute sense of smell and is very agile, breaking into an amazing sprint when it sights its prey, and in pursuit is able to leap over obstacles 2m (6ft) high.

Flora and Fauna

An Ibizan boast is that there is absolutely nothing dangerous on the island: no snakes, nasty insects, poisonous plants or savage animals. And, apart from the odd wasp and mosquito, this is largely true. Flora and fauna which do exist include a mixture of cultivated fruit trees, imported by **Carthaginians** and **Romans**; an abundance of wild herbs and flowers; and several species of bird, lizard and small mammal.

In spring, Ibiza is carpeted with a magnificent display of wild flowers. Olive orchards stand knee-deep in scarlet poppies and brilliant blue cornflowers, and hedgerows are bursting with cow parsley and pink and yellow blooms. Orange and lemon trees are heavy with fruit while wild rosemary and thyme scent the air. Other cultivated trees include vast ancient figs, brilliant-green carob and almond, and there are wild pines all over the island. Wheat, potatoes, tomatoes, onions, garlic and vines are grown.

As well as the many lizards – some a brilliant shade of green – Ibiza is home to hedgehogs, squirrels, rabbits, and hares, among others. Several species of migratory bird call in at the salt flats of Ses Salines in the south and owls can be heard hooting in the woods at night. Birds of prey are hard to spot but do exist and at **Cala d'Hort** in the south, rare Eleanora falcons can be seen wheeling in the sky.

Opposite: *In spring the landscape bursts alive with brilliant displays of poppies.*
Above: *Thick bunches of black grapes hang heavy on the vine during summer.*
Below: *The Ibizenco breed of dog, Ca Eivissenc, has an unusually acute sense of smell.*

HISTORY IN BRIEF

The development of Ibiza and Formentera has been quite separate from that of their Balearic neighbours, Mallorca and Menorca. While there is evidence of prehistoric settlers at **Ca Na Costa** on Formentera from 2000BC, the Pitiusas have far fewer megalithic sites today than the other Balearic islands.

TANIT

The Carthaginians' goddess of sexuality, Tanit, was worshipped in sanctuaries all over Ibiza, one of the most important being **Es Cuieram** in the mountains overlooking Cala Sant Vicent. As well as representing love and fertility, Tanit's more sinister side was as the goddess of the dead. The Greeks, who hated the Carthaginians, told stories of human sacrifices made to Tanit, which included children and young virgins, and of prostitution conducted by priests. Symbols associated with Tanit include the dove, the fruit of the pomegranate tree and the moon. Signs of the goddess have been found on amulets of bronze, ivory and bone and can be seen in the archaeological museum.

Carthaginians

Ibiza became a colony of Carthage in 700BC. The Carthaginians were a powerful race of traders and merchants from North Africa who, drawn by its valuable resources of salt and lead, called in at Ibiza en route to mainland Spain. Discovering something of a paradise, an island of great beauty and no natural hazards, the Carthaginians settled, even bringing their dead in the belief that the island would be an ideal setting in which to enter the afterlife. The necropolis at **Puig des Molins** outside Eivissa was developed as a result and provides many valuable insights today into the Carthaginian lifestyle.

Under the influence of Carthage, Ibiza became in effect an outpost of North Africa. **Hannibal**, the famous Carthaginian general allegedly born on Ibiza, was defeated by the **Romans** in 202BC during the Second Punic War but, even after the subsequent fall of Carthage in 146BC, Ibiza remained more Carthaginian than Roman, enjoying an autonomy denied to Mallorca and Menorca and the

Right: *Archaeologists view the Carthaginian tomb at Ca Na Costa on Formentera as an example of architecture well ahead of its time.*
Opposite: *Traces of Roman presence on Ibiza, though minimal, remain. Headless statues flank the main gate to Eivissa's Dalt Vila. These are copies of original pieces now kept in the archaeological museum.*

Spanish mainland. Special Ibizenco coins from this era can be seen in the archaeological museum.

The Romans, like their predecessors, exploited the island's salt and lead and made olive oil and wine from the fruits of the countryside. They also made *garum*, a special, pungent sauce containing fermented fish innards, considered a great delicacy at the time.

By the 5th century AD, the Roman Empire had begun to decline and a peaceful, productive era came to an abrupt end when the **Vandals**, an aggressive tribe from northern Europe, invaded Spain and quickly occupied Ibiza and Formentera. Little was documented about this period and scant archaeological evidence remains today.

The next big cultural influence on the island was the **Moors**, who ousted the **Christian Byzantines** who had briefly replaced the unpopular Vandals. Consisting of amalgamated tribes from North Africa united by Islam, the Moors arrived in mainland Spain in AD711 and by AD905 had conquered the Balearics. A period of relative calm followed on Ibiza, during which the island was developed for agriculture. Formentera, wide open to pirate attack with its long, exposed beaches, was only sparsely populated. Once again, surprisingly little remains from this era other than a few place names, some words in the Ibizenco dialect, and assorted ceramics. The inland village of **Balafi** is probably the only surviving example of Moorish architecture on Ibiza.

The Moors hung on to parts of Spain for some 300 years, incorporating Ibiza into the **Caliphate of Córdoba** and later, the **Taifas** (small kingdoms) of **Denia** and then **Mallorca**. They were briefly ousted by the more zealous Islamic tribes of the **Almoravides** and then **Almohades**. But the Christians were gradually reconquering Spain and, on 8 August 1235, Ibiza was taken by the forces of Guillem de Montgrí, Nuno Sans and Prince Pedro of Portugal, on behalf of **King Jaume I of Catalunya**. After a bloody battle, the Catalan troops entered the walled city of Eivissa and the Moors were driven out of the island.

NOSTRADAMUS

A 15th-century French astrologer, Nostradamus, predicted various astonishing world events by gazing into a glass of water. Thousands of his visions are documented in a best-selling book. His prophecies included the assassination of President Kennedy, the activities of Adolf Hitler and the Gulf War. Quite bizarrely, the tiny island of Ibiza featured in one of his blackest predictions, that life on Earth would virtually be wiped out by nuclear war. Only the unusual prevailing wind pattern over Ibiza would save the island and its people from extinction: 'Ibiza will be Earth's final refuge'.

Historical Calendar

2000BC Neolithic era. People arrive by primitive boat from the mainland.
7th century BC Late Bronze Age. Carthaginians arrive and settle. Puig des Molins developed as a necropolis.
218–201BC Second Punic war. Hannibal defeated.
123BC Mallorca and Menorca occupied by Rome.
AD74 Ibiza becomes part of the province of Tarragona.
426 Vandals from northern Europe defeat Romans.
903 Moorish conquest of Balearics complete.
1235 Forces of King Jaume I of Catalunya reconquer Ibiza.
1492 Columbus discovers America; importance of Mediterranean declines.
16th–17th centuries Poverty, plague and Barbary pirate raids plunge Pitiusas into destitution. Formentera too dangerous for settlement.
1715 Islanders' rights to the saltpans removed after Napoleonic wars.
1936–38 Spanish Civil War. Ibiza supports Franco.
1960 Hippies discover Ibiza.
1975 Juan Carlos I becomes ruler of Spain after death of Franco. Tourism expands.
1983 Ibiza and Formentera become part of the autonomous community of the Balearics.
1986 Spain joins European Community, which later becomes European Union.
1998 Britain's consul-general in Ibiza resigns, disgusted by loutish behaviour of certain British tourists.
2000 Ibiza receives 2m visitors and achieves cult status as Europe's clubbing capital.

Opposite top: *El Obelisco a los Corsarios in the Sa Marina district of Eivissa.*
Opposite bottom: *Formidable bastions were built around Eivissa's Dalt Vila in the 16th century.*

Columbus

Christopher Columbus (b. 1451) sailed west from Spain in 1492, hoping to discover a new route to Asia. Instead, he landed on a small island in the Bahamas and went on over the next five years to discover Cuba, Jamaica, Venezuela, Panama and what is now Haiti and the Dominican Republic. Columbus never actually set foot on what is now the USA; the closest he got was Puerto Rico, for which he continues to get the credit for having discovered America. He died in 1506.

Christianity

Christianity and the Catalan language were established on Ibiza, which was divided into four areas: **Yabisa** (now Eivissa), **Portmany** (now Sant Antoni), **Ses Salines** and **Santa Eulària**. A church (now the cathedral) was built in honour of Santa Maria and smaller churches were constructed at Santa Eulària, Sant Antoni, Sant Miquel and Sant Jordi.

Another period of historical oblivion followed. Although a governing body, **La Universitat**, had been established and the new Catalan nobility had made considerable investment in Eivissa town, ceaseless pirate raids and an epidemic of plague in 1348 turned Ibiza into a backwater. From around 1403, Formentera was uninhabited, so severe was the threat from pirates. Mainland Spain was turning its attention to the New World, which had been reached by **Columbus** in 1492, but the spoils barely reached the forgotten islands of the Mediterranean.

Much of the island's architecture today bears witness to the constant raids by Barbary pirates from North Africa. Round, stone towers – many of them still standing – were built as lookouts. Tough, fortified churches were constructed on hilltops, providing a refuge for the peasants in the event of an attack. Eivissa was fortified and

other villages developed inland, away from the exposed coast. A band of semi-legal vigilantes, the **Corsarios**, emerged, local heroes who fought back at the pirates, raiding their ships and 'stealing' the loot.

After the **War of Spanish Succession** (1702–14) Ibiza became part of the province of the Balearics and Castilian Spanish became the official language. Having backed the eventual loser in the war, Ibiza was forced to give up control of its saltpans as punishment and numerous islanders became bankrupt. Many Ibizencos emigrated while Formentera continued to be uninhabited.

Civil War

Spain's fortunes declined dramatically in the early 20th century. All the American colonies had been lost, the then king, **Alfonso XIII**, went into exile and in 1936 the country fell into civil war. Ibiza, Formentera and Menorca, together with Andalucia, Navarra, Galicia and parts of Castille, supported **General Francisco Franco**'s Nationalist troops but all the major population centres were Republican.

The rest of the world was quick to take sides. Germany and Italy supported Franco, supplying him with troops and munitions. The Soviet Union, meanwhile, called for communists and socialists to unite against fascism. The Republicans received sporadic aid from this brief liaison, though Stalin eventually abandoned the cause.

CORSARIOS

Corsarios, or privateers, were certified by the crown in 1356 to challenge pirate ships if they were seen as a threat to the mother country. The crown took one-fifth of the spoils and the privateer kept the rest. Without the corsairs, Ibiza's economy would have been considerably weaker as the raids on pirate ships brought otherwise unaffordable consumer goods to the islands.

Locals enjoy the legend of **Antoni Riguer**, a fearless corsair who in 1806 captured the ship *Felicity*, commanded by a Gibraltarian pirate. Riguer achieved this from the flimsiest of *feluccas* (a wooden sailing boat) and the battle which raged out at sea could be heard all over the islands. A monument to the corsairs stands in the port of Eivissa today, erected in 1915 after their activities were prohibited in 1908.

During the civil war over 600,000 lives were lost in bombings, executions, starvation and disease. All over Spain churches and cathedrals were burned down by Republicans, and mass killing was known to be carried out by the Nationalists. Horrific bombing raids wiped out entire towns. While the Balearics suffered less than mainland Spain, the war affected the economy and morale of the whole country which, destitute and emotionally shattered, limped into the middle of the century under the victorious Franco.

Above: *The hippie trail in the 1960s brought new influences to the islands, including colourful goods from Goa.*

Famous Names

Artists and actors flocked to Ibiza in the swinging '60s and many have left their legacy. Terry Thomas's house is still there, as is the home of the late Denholm Elliot and his wife. Ursula Andress lived here, as did Diana Rigg, Ali McGraw, Terence Stamp and Peter Sellers. Top models who holiday here include Linda Evangelista and Elle MacPherson. Nicki Lauda, Boris Becker and Paul Young all visit regularly, as do Brad Pitt, director Roman Polanski and Mick Hucknall of Simply Red. The guest book at Pikes, a celebrity-studded hotel outside Sant Antoni, is a modern Who's Who: Tony Curtis, Julio Iglesias, Sade and Bon Jovi are all regulars.

The Hippie Era

During the 1960s, an entirely new kind of visitor arrived. Despite the fact that Franco and Prohibition were very much in evidence on the mainland, Ibiza was far enough from Madrid to enjoy relative freedom. **Hippies** from California began to visit en route from Marrakech in Morocco to Goa, spending carefree summers in Ibiza. Artists and designers were quick to follow and Ibiza soon developed an internationally known style of its own, **Ad Lib**. The arrival of Europe's rich, famous and beautiful on this new-found paradise spawned exotic nightlife, which more recently evolved into Europe's hottest club scene.

In the 1970s, the advent of charter flights and wide-bodied jets meant the birth of the package holiday. Having successfully secured a niche, Ibiza continues today to attract a more modern kind of hippie and an exotic summer culture of wealthy yacht owners. The less attractive face of mass-market tourism has unquestionably scarred the landscape in places but much of the island remains blissfully unspoiled.

GOVERNMENT AND ECONOMY

In 1982 the **Socialist Worker's Party** (PSOE), led by Felipe Gonzales, was elected. The socialist government successfully integrated Spain into the **European Community** (now European Union) in 1986 and the country continued to recover economically, putting itself in the world spotlight in 1992 with the Expo in Seville, the Olympics in Barcelona and the European City of Culture in Madrid all in the same year. In 1996, the PSOE was ousted by the **Partido Popular** led by **Mario Aznar**, which holds a small majority and faces ongoing issues of unemployment as well as the task of bringing Spain's economy and standard of living in line with the more powerful nations of the European Union.

The Balearic Islands – Mallorca, Menorca, Ibiza and Formentera – have been one of Spain's 17 autonomous regions since 1983. **Palma**, capital of Mallorca, is also the regional capital and seat of government of the Balearics. Mallorca has 33 seats, Menorca 12, Ibiza 11 and Formentera three. The two dominant parties, the PSOE and PP-UM (Partido Popular-Union Mallorquina) account for 75% of the votes.

The total population of the islands is 745,000, of whom just 73,000 live on Ibiza. Tiny Formentera only has a population of 5000.

Education in Spain is compulsory from the ages of six to 16 and young men have to do national service. There is no university in Ibiza; the nearest one is in Palma. Before the advent of tourism, both islands were extremely poor and their only exports were salt, onions and potatoes. Now, Ibiza exports 60,000 tonnes of salt annually, although more advanced mechanization has meant that the saltpans provide only a handful of jobs. Almost everybody else works in tourism or a tourism-related industry.

NAMES FOR THE ISLANDS

Ibiza and Formentera have been given many different names over the centuries. The Greeks once called them **Gimnesias** – islands of the nudes – or Aphrodite Islands, in the belief that goddesses emerged from the waves. More lasting was **Pitiusas**, or Pine Islands. By the 5th century BC, the town of Eivissa was known as **Ebusim**, coming from the name of the god Bes. The Moors, who invaded Spain in AD711, called the island **Yabisha**. Formentera, meanwhile, was called **Ophiussa** – island of serpents – by the Greeks, despite the fact that there were no snakes. Later, its name was derived from *frumentum*, the Latin for 'wheat'.

Below: *Salt production remains an important industry, though the provision of free salt to islanders has ceased.*

Catalan Pronunciation

Catalan, of which Eivissenc is a dialect, is mystifying to anyone who has just mastered basic Castilian Spanish as it's completely different, even though some words have a similar root. Here are a few of the more peculiar pronunciations:

- **g** followed by **e** or **i** is pronounced like 'zh' in 'Zhivago'
- **ig** is pronounced like 'tch' in 'hatch'
- **n** before an **f** or a **v** is sometimes pronounced 'm'
- **r** is rolled at the beginning of a word and usually silent at the end
- **v** at the beginning of a word is pronounced 'b', and 'f' elsewhere
- **w** is pronounced either as a 'v' or a 'b'
- **x** is pronounced 'sh' in most words.

THE PEOPLE

Ibizenco people are by nature both industrious and easy-going. The reason the island is so popular with Europe's famous, rich and outrageous is because of the amazing tolerance of Ibiza's population, who regard the summer carnival of visitors with an open mind. The hippie invasion of the late 1960s was an eye-opener for these simple farmers but was nonetheless politely tolerated in the rather false hope that the hippies would contribute something to Ibiza's flagging economy. The tourists who followed hot on the hippies' heels were also welcomed and the islanders took enthusiastically to constructing a tourism industry.

Family ties are strong in Ibiza and Formentera and land is kept in the same family for years, even if generations have left the islands. Both islands are predominantly Roman Catholic and the local church forms the focal point of each community, despite the fact that the islanders like to build their *fincas* (farms) spread out across the countryside.

Local festivals are celebrated with tremendous flair and, given the cultural impositions from British and German tourists that locals in Sant Antoni and Es Canar have to put up with, Ibiza has a remarkable grip on its cultural heritage.

Below: *Preparations for the festival of Santa Maria de las Neus.*

Ibiza and, to a lesser extent, Formentera, also have large expatriate communities of seasonal workers, who come flooding in from Britain, Germany and Scandinavia in search of their own slice of Ibizenco magic. Those who found it in the 1960s, now middle-aged hippies, have settled around the pretty town of **Sant Carles**.

Language

Above: *Rivalry at a brass band competition on Passeig Vara del Rey, festival time.*

Catalan or its local dialect, **Eivissenc**, is undergoing a strong revival. In remote villages, the dialect has always been spoken, despite being banned under Franco. While Castilian Spanish continues to be taught in schools, road signs, some newspapers and conversation are now generally in Catalan. This book uses the Eivissenc version of a place name wherever it has been converted on the islands. English and German are widely spoken in bars and restaurants on both islands but locals are always delighted to be addressed in their own language.

Festivals

Regular festivals to celebrate saints' days are one of the only things keeping traditional culture alive. These are celebrated with gusto and present an opportunity to admire the costumes and dances peculiar to the island, and to listen to the songs of old fishermen.

As every village has a different saint's day, there's a good chance most visitors will be able to join in some kind of celebration. A typical day will involve demonstrations of traditional dancing in a village square decked with coloured bunting, followed by a slow march out into the countryside with the parade bearing an effigy of the saint in question. The dancing, feasting and drinking continues into the night.

The big celebrations, however, are **Carnival** in February, **Semana Santa**, or Holy Week, in the week before Easter, **May Day** in Santa Eulària, and 4–8 August in Eivissa. During this week, the saint's day of **Santa Maria de las Neus**, our Lady of the Snows and patron saint of Ibiza, is celebrated with a series of parades, fireworks displays, a special mass, concerts and street performances.

Main Festivals

February • Carnival
March • Semana Santa – Holy Week: processions in Eivissa and Santa Eulària on the night of Good Friday
First Sunday in May • Flower festival in Santa Eulària
23–24 June • Sant Joan de Labritja: fireworks, bonfires and celebrations in Eivissa and Sant Antoni
16 July • Virgen del Carmen: regattas in Eivissa
25 July • San Jaime: processions, singing and dancing on Formentera
4–8 August • Santa Maria de las Neus: the biggest festival of the year with five days of fireworks and parties in honour of Eivissa's patron
1 November • All Saints Day: special cakes and pastries sold in Ibiza and Formentera

Carnival in February is a big, pre-lenten celebration of costume parades and parties, while Semana Santa before Easter is a more sombre affair, with candelit processions and special masses. Santa Eulària's **flower festival** takes place on the first Sunday in May, which usually coincides with the start of the holiday season. There's a parade of horse-drawn carriages, each vehicle decked with garlands of flowers; flower competitions; dancing and marching bands. Everybody turns out to watch the parade, eat cakes and tapas from roadside stalls and swig sangria or wine from a *porron*, a traditional drinking vessel with a long spout.

The August celebrations actually begin at the end of July with a swim across the harbour from **Sa Marina** to **Botafoch**. There are fireworks on 1 August, dancing and funfairs on the 5th and a mass and floral offerings to the Virgin on the 6th. On the 6th there's also a quayside ceremony in honour of the corsairs, Ibiza's one-time privateers. The festival culminates with processions and dancing on the 8th. The whole of **Passeig Vara del Rey**, the most beautiful street in Eivissa, comes alive with dancing and street performances.

Traditional Dancing

Ibizenco dancing, or *ball pagés*, dates back to 1000BC and is a special feature of local festivals. Based on old pagan fertility rights, it is quite unlike anything on the mainland. The dances are thought to stem from rituals of worship to the Carthaginian goddess, Tanit, and take place by wells, fountains and water wheels, where the running water represents life.
There are five basic steps: *curta* (short), where the woman makes circular movements facing the man, who performs a series of leaps; *larga* (long), with a faster rhythm; *safilera* (in a row); *ses dotze rodades*, or the twelve turns; and the *filera*, a special dance performed at weddings by the bride and bridesmaids.

Nightlife

No one can fail to experience the legendary nightlife of Ibiza. From June to the end of September, people flock to the island for a sample of celebrated nightclubs like **Privilege**, **Pacha** and **Amnesia**, vast caverns with amazing special effects and top DJs brought in from the mainland and the UK. Even if you're not a clubber, a *passeig* (or stroll) in the Sa Marina district of Eivissa is floorshow enough. The two main centres of nightlife are **Eivissa** – for people-watching, expensive cocktails and the hippest bars – and **Sant Antoni**, which attracts a younger crowd. The two biggest clubs, Privilege (which holds 9000) and Amnesia, are opposite one another on the Eivissa-Sant Antoni road. Pacha is in Eivissa and **Space**, which doesn't even open until 06:00, is in Platja d'en Bossa.

Start the night at sunset with a *passeig* through the town and a few cocktails. The places to be seen are Base and The Rock on Carrer Garijo, or Dome, which combines glamour with the gay crowd. After having dinner in one of the backstreets at around 22:00, spend some time watching the people again on their second, alcohol-fuelled *passeig*, generally wandering towards one of the nightclubs.

No self-respecting clubber would turn up before 01:00 and everything only really gets going towards 02:00. In Eivissa, Pacha is the place to be seen and will operate a door policy on busy nights, so dress the part. Anything outrageous, but definitely not scruffy, will do. The incredibly wealthy sit sipping vintage champagne in roped-off areas away from the masses.

All the clubs stay open until dawn when the truly dedicated move on to Space at 06:00. Here it's possible to ignore the sunlight outside and dance until midday before collapsing under a sun umbrella to sleep.

Nightlife Alternatives

There's more to Ibiza than clubs. Here are a few ideas:

- Soak up the atmosphere of the races at the **Hippodrome**.
- Try your luck at the **Casino** in Eivissa.
- Listen to live **jazz** at the Pereira café in Eivissa.
- Watch a **movie** in the rather quaint cinema of Santa Eulària (films screened once a week in English).
- Wander round the **shops and market** in Sa Marina until late.
- Go **ten-pin bowling** in Sant Antoni.

Opposite: *Traditional dancing is still very much alive, as here at the village of Sant Miquel.*

Below: *Foam parties and drag shows are a feature of the big clubs.*

THE PASSEIG

The *passeig* – an evening walk or stroll – is an essential component of Spanish nightlife in the summer months. After the sun has set, everybody slowly parades the island's trendiest areas, stopping for tapas and to greet friends. A second *passeig* takes place between tapas and dinner, usually around 23:00, after which most people repair to a bar and then a nightclub. The best locations for people-watching are the Cafe Montesol in Eivissa, busy all day long with outdoor tables and chairs; the outdoor tables at Vogue, Tango and Zoo in the 'Ibiza Triangle'; anywhere on the seafront of Sant Antoni's West End; and around the marina in Santa Eulària.

Gay Ibiza

Ibiza has for some time been a magnet for gay holidaymakers and enjoys a lively, uninhibited and relaxed scene. Gay life is concentrated around Eivissa and there are several bars and clubs serving a predominantly gay clientele.

Outside the walls of Dalt Vila, the **Carrer Mare de Déu** in the old fishing quarter of **Sa Penya** has a good concentration of bars. Benidorm, Broux and Catwalk are all popular, while Teatro is a legendary drag bar. Below the floodlit walls of the old town, Incognito on **Carrer Santa Llúcia** has a beautiful terrace while Lolas, close by, is one of the island's original clubs.

Inside Dalt Vila, **Sa Carossa** is the hub of the gay scene with a great atmosphere and plenty of venues, such as Camp Nonsense, a kitsch hangout with a glittery disco ball. Also try Dome where the action gets going at 01:00 as people parade down Carrer Alfonso XII before heading to the clubs. For those in search of a quiet meal on the beach away from the madding crowd, Chiringay on **Platja d'Es Cavallet** is good fun. There are plenty of gay-friendly hotels, as well. The Marigna Hotel in **Figueretas**, for example, is exclusively for gay and lesbian holidaymakers.

Below: *Eivissa teems with nightlife possibilities.*

Architecture

Above: *Ibizenco houses have a distinctive style.*

Ibiza's minimalist, eye-catching rural architecture has been copied all over the world, something of an irony as it stems from simple peasant houses with no plans and no designers. Country houses were built in a simple cube shape so that more cubes could easily be added as the family expanded. Walls were thick to preserve cool air and windows tiny to keep out the burning sun. Socializing took place on the shaded porch (*porxet*) which was also used for the storage of fruit and vegetables. Roofs were flat and waterproofed with charcoal, clay and dried seaweed, and a well and clay oven were usually located outside. Today, the division and redivision of property means that the whole island is crisscrossed with low, stone walls. Each square is known as a *tanques* and each house has a tiny walled garden, or *es tancó*, with a few vegetables and palm trees and the occasional, dazzling bougainvillea or hibiscus.

Many great architects have taken inspiration from the simplicity of Ibizenco houses. Walter Gropius, the founder of the Bauhaus movement, the great cubist Le Corbusier, Josep Lluis Sert and Erwin Broner all spent time here from the 1950s onwards and a lot of the luxurious villas that were built in the 1970s have adhered to the theme. But to see the prettiest original Ibizenco houses, walk out into the countryside around **Sant Carles** or climb the hill outside Santa Eulària to the little church surrounded by a cluster of dazzling sugar cubes.

Art and Fashion

The bright, clear light and vivid colours of Ibiza have inspired many foreign artists to take root here and paint. There are certainly some excellent galleries in Eivissa town and the **Museu d'Art Contemporani** (Museum of Contemporary Art) in Eivissa's Dalt Vila has a good and

Contemporary Art

While the Balearic islands have bred no international names in the art world, the light and scenery attracts legions of good professionals and semi-professionals as well as countless *domingueros* – Sunday painters. A growing market of wealthy people looking for 'island style' with which to furnish their luxury Ibizenco villas sustains a number of good galleries, mainly in Eivissa. Look out for the work of Mallorcan painter **Miguel Barceló** and local artist **Jussara Heberle**. Galleries for serious buyers include **Galeria Carl van der Voort** and **Sa Nostra** in Eivissa; **Elefante** and **Es Moli** outside Santa Gertrudis; and **Punta A** and **Can Daita** in Santa Gertudis itself.

varied programme of exhibitions of local artists, changing every two months. But the work on sale to tourists generally includes a fair amount of sentimental trash interspersed with a few good watercolours of Ibizenco village scenes, so buy from a good gallery.

Something unique is Ibizenco fashion. The hippie era gave rise to a local style which imitated the traditional women's wear on the island. This evolved into a world-famous line of summer wear, under the label **Ad Lib**. Founded by the late **Smilya Mihailovitch**, an icon of Ibizenco high society, Ad Lib's trademark is floaty whites in lace and cotton with the occasional splash of vivid colour, evolving, the designer said, from the *laissez faire* hippie culture and the desire in the 1970s to break free from Parisian *haute couture*. There are several shops in Eivissa town selling Ad Lib and a packed-out fashion show attended by the world's fashion press, **Moda Ad Lib**, is held in various locations around the island every summer. Another local label, **Papillon**, has a tiny boutique in the sleepy village of Sant Carles, home of the original hippie movement.

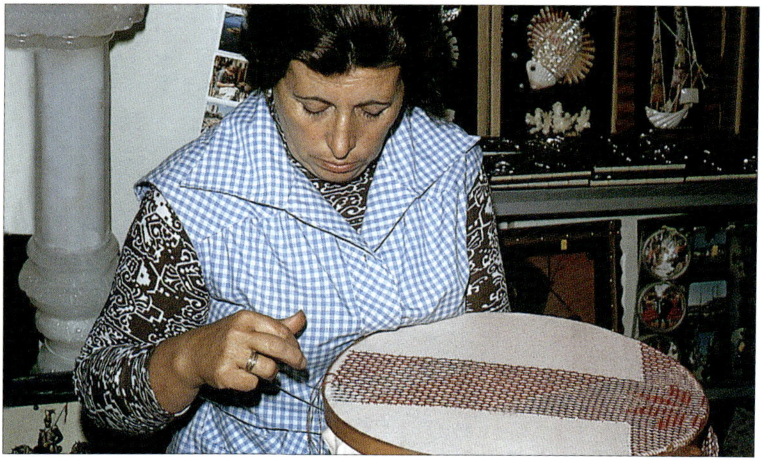

Food

Ibizenco cuisine reflects the island's somewhat impoverished past when people lived a simple existence off the land. Rich stews, hearty soups, game, Mediterranean vegetables and spicy sausages are all regular features of a gastronomic tradition that reflects subsistence farming rather than *haute cuisine.*

An old Ibizenco saying that is loosely translated as 'any bird that flies, gets put in the pot' no longer holds true, although songbirds like thrushes and starlings are considered a delicacy and do feature in local cookbooks. Meat dishes on the island tend to revolve around chicken, pork and occasionally lamb, with the odd game dish of partridge or rabbit.

The real highlight of eating in Ibiza is the fish, served in a hundred different ways and deliciously fresh. Seafood lovers should try **paella**, not an Ibizenco dish but originating from Valencia on the mainland. It has become something of an island tradition to head off to a beach restaurant for Sunday lunch and get through several bottles of *rosado* (rosé wine) and a giant pan of paella, rich with succulent prawns, mussels, clams, squid and crayfish. Alternatively, restaurants will bring out their catch of the day to show you and present a variety of ways for it to be prepared.

Ibizenco Cuisine

Several cookbooks feature the cuisine of the Balearics and make a good souvenir. If you try to recreate those favourite holiday dishes at home, however, you may find some of the ingredients hard to come by! Country stew, for example, requires 10 starlings, while Milky Autumn Rice demands one partridge, one woodcock, a rabbit and three starlings. For meat balls, you'll need 100g (3½ oz) of golden thistles, and for stuffed turkey, a pig's ear. Pigeon with wild mushrooms requires 'four fat pigeons that have not left the nest', and Stuffed Thrushes 'eight fat thrushes from the olive woods'. But don't worry; plenty of the dishes are more manageable!

Opposite top: *The shops of Eivissa do a fine line in fashionable summer wear.*
Opposite bottom: *Crafts such as glass-making and embroidery are kept up in inland villages.*
Left: *Paella, mainstay of Spanish cuisine, is equally popular on Ibiza and Formentera.*

Right: *Vegetarian options are also available, making full use of Mediterranean ingedients.*
Opposite: *Dried hams hang above the counter at Can Costa bar in Santa Gertrudis.*

TYPICAL TAPAS

Tapas are usually displayed under a glass case at the bar so, as a last resort, you can point but it always helps to understand the menu. Menus are presented in Castilian and Catalan and the following are tapas typical of the area:
***Albóndigas*:** meatballs in sauce
Anchoas (Catalan: ***Anxoves***): anchovies
***Boquerones*:** fresh anchovies fried in a light batter, highly recommended
***Caracoles*:** snails, usually in a spicy sauce
***Chorizo*:** spicy sausage
***Croqueta*:** fish or chicken croquettes
***Gambas*:** shrimp
***Mejillones*:** mussels
***Patatas bravas*:** sautéed potatoes in a spicy sauce
Tortilla (Catalan: ***Truita***): Spanish omelette.

One thing every fish-lover ought to try is *guixat de peix*, a speciality of Ibiza and an absolute feast. Firm fish such as red snapper is cooked slowly with potatoes, garlic, onion, tomatoes, plenty of saffron, cinammon, olive oil and salt. The resulting huge platter of fish and potatoes is served as a first course and then as a second course, the remaining stock is used to cook wonderfully fragrant rice in a kind of soup, rich with shellfish. Squid is also very popular, either *a la plancha* (grilled) or stewed with rice in its own ink. For a really meaty fish dish, *toyina a l'eivissenca* is delicious and consists of tuna prepared with pine nuts, raisins, eggs, spices, lemon juice, and white wine.

Local meat dishes include *sofrit pagés*, a kind of stew made from fried sausages (*sobrassada* and *botifarrons*) simmered with potatoes, spices and saffron, and *frita pagesa*, a mixture of fried pork and pork liver added to red peppers, mushrooms, garlic and potatoes. Game is quite popular: *perdius am col* is partridge with cabbage, and *conill amb pebrots vermelles* is rabbit with red peppers.

Vegetarians

The Balearic islands have not really understood the concept of vegetarianism yet and it is not unusual for non-fish or meat eaters to be offered prawns or snails as an alternative! With a bit of effort, however, vegetari-

ans can dine well. Look out for huge salads topped with egg, avocado and pine nuts; *olla fresca*, a delicious stew of mixed beans and potatoes with spices; and *truita*, commonly known as Spanish omelette. In Formentera, try the local cheeses, made from sheep or goat's milk. Good tapas bars on both islands serve plenty of vegetarian options.

Sweets and Desserts

Several local pastries are worth exploring. *Ensaimadas* are light cakes filled with cream, almond paste or preserves while *greixonera* are biscuits flavoured with cinammon or lemon. Aniseed is used to flavour *orietes* cakes. In May and June fresh fruit is delicious and *fresas con nata* – strawberries with cream – is served everywhere (although the cream is usually the spray-on variety). Year round, try a delicious export from Catalunya on the mainland, *crema catalana*, a kind of *crème brûlée* served hot with a caramelized top.

VEGETARIAN SURVIVAL

Vegetarianism is not widely appreciated in the Balearics but there are a few things to choose from the menu. Useful phrases include: 'Sóc vegetarià/iana' or 'Non puc menjar carn' (I can't eat meat). There are plenty of pizza restaurants in the main tourist resorts as well as Indian and Chinese, all of which serve vegetarian options. Rincon de Pepe in Santa Eulària makes a fantastic range of veggie tapas, including grilled Mediterranean vegetables, stuffed courgettes, garlic grilled mushrooms, spinach with raisins, Russian salad and aubergine stew.

International cuisine

Bland 'international cuisine' is everywhere in Ibiza and Formentera's holiday resorts. British visitors can dine happily on roast beef and Yorkshire pudding while Germans will find restaurants specializing in *wurst* and *sauerkraut*. Pizza and pasta establishments abound, some of them very good, and there are a few Chinese and Indian restaurants.

Drinks

Straggly vines eke out an existence in Ibiza's sun-drenched fields but their produce is something of a rarity. If you stop for lunch somewhere particularly rustic, you may get to sample Ibizenco wine but don't expect to find it in the best restaurants. The name, *vi de taula pagés* (peasant wine), speaks for itself.

On Formentera, the hearty country reds are slightly more palatable. Excellent wines from mainland Spain are available everywhere and rosé, the poor relation of white, is particularly fashionable to drink with tapas. **Riojas** and **Navarras**, as well as **Codorniu** and **Freixenet** cava sparkling wines, are priced very reasonably and worth sampling.

What Ibiza does specialize in is *hierbas*, a kind of digestif made locally by most of the better restaurants. *Frigola* is sold everywhere, a concoction of thyme and wildflowers steeped in any liqueur. More authentic still is a nameless liqueur in which sprigs of rosemary, fennel, mint, juniper berries and even pine needles are marinated in anise. The result tastes sweet and fragrant and apparently has excellent digestive properties.

Sangría is another local favourite, drunk all over Spain with tapas and at picnics. Beware of its potency: the combination of red wine, brandy, fruit and ice slips down easily and if you're not careful, in vast quantities. Otherwise, *cerveza* (beer) comes in bottles and ranges from the renowned **San Miguel** to foreign imports. Spirits are served in enormous measures (compared, at least, to

CAVA PRODUCTION

While on Ibiza, try the excellent sparkling wines (*cavas*) made on the mainland, just outside Barcelona. To make *cava*, grapes are fermented and the resulting base mixed with sugar and yeast. The bottles are corked and laid flat in the cellar for a second fermentation and the wine later decanted so that sediment is removed before the final corking. There are four levels of sweetness: *brut*, the driest; *sec*; *semi-sec*; and *dolc*, best drunk as a dessert wine. Good *cavas* to drink are Ana Codorníu, Codorníu's Première Cuvée Brut, Freixenet's Cordon Negro (in its characteristic black bottles), Brut Nature, and Reserva Real.

those in Britain and the USA); local brands, like Larios gin, are cheaper than imports. **Jerez**, the famous Spanish sherry produced in Andalucía, is also drunk as an aperitif, although less so than on the mainland. Ask for *fino*, a fine, straw-coloured wine, served chilled.

Nonalcoholic drinks include *granizados* (fruit juice over crushed ice) and, of course, coffee, drunk *con leche* (with hot milk) in the mornings, and French-style or *sólo* (black) at other times. If you ask for *descafeinado* (decaffeinated) it comes with hot milk and in a Nescafé sachet.

Ibizan tap water, with all due respect, is extremely unpleasant. Most of it comes from artesian wells and is both salty and strong with chemicals. Limestone makes it very hard so don't be surprised if soap and shampoo seem virtually ineffective. Bottled water is available everywhere, either *con gas* (sparkling) or *sin gas* (still).

Spanish Sporting Stars

The fact that tennis, golf and cycling are national passions in Spain is no surprise, given the success of Spanish sporting stars in these fields. Arantxa Sanchez Vicario, Conchita Martinez and Alberto Berasategui dominate the international tennis circuit, while Seve Ballesteros and Jose Maria Olazábel are two of the world's great golfers. Miguel Indurain, meanwhile, is a national hero for his multiple wins of the Tour de France and visitors to Ibiza and Formentera will often have to make way on the secondary roads for groups of racing cyclists speeding along in brightly coloured Lycra.

Sport

A balmy climate and safe, gently sloping beaches make Ibiza perfect for learning a new sport. Most of the larger beaches like **Ses Salines** and **Es Cavallet** have windsurfing schools, as well as dinghies and catamarans for hire. **Formentera**, meanwhile, with wide, open sands and good strong winds attracts the real windsurfing aficionados. Waterskiing and jetskiing are less popular than the wind-powered sports, which makes for peaceful sunbathing. There are, however, plenty of 'banana boats' – long, rubber inflatables towed behind a motorboat and ridden by whooping holidaymakers. At the quieter beaches, pedalos can be hired but beware – a pedalo can be a recipe for sunburn. Also, remember to allow enough time to get back to the beach if you've rented a pedalo by the hour.

Opposite: Hierbas, *an interesting concoction of liqueur and herbs, is a local speciality.*

Below: *For messing around in the water, banana boats take some beating. Ibiza's waters are generally relatively quiet.*

MARINE LIFE

The local claim that 'nothing on Ibiza bites or stings' doesn't hold true for the sea, where a few minor hazards lurk. Spiky black **sea urchins** lie scattered over the rocks but the water is so clear that their presence shouldn't be a problem. Small **jellyfish** can sting, although an anti-insect-bite spray usually eases the pain. Also to be avoided is the **spider crab**, **spiny dog-fish**, **thornback ray** and **red dragonhead**. Everything else is relatively harmless and usually edible. Monkfish, tuna and sea bass inhabit the deeper waters.

Scuba Diving

There are some sensational dive sites around the coasts of Ibiza and Formentera. The government protects the island's ecological and archaeological heritage fiercely and all divers must have a special licence from **CRIS** (Centro de Recuperación y Investigaciones Submarines), the underwater research and discovery centre. Old coins and ampoules must not be removed and spear-fishing is forbidden.

There are currently 14 dive centres on Ibiza which will guide visiting divers over wrecks and caves to view marine life such as barracuda, grouper, slipper lobster, sunfish and rainbows of coral in visibility of up to 40m (130ft). All divers have access to the decompression chamber on the island. Tuition is available at most of the dive schools and Ibiza is a perfect place to learn – you can be fully qualified in five days.

Opposite and below: *Yachting is popular around Ibiza and Formentera and opportunities for taking up scuba diving are ample.*

Golf

Ibiza has 27 holes of golf at **Roca Llisa** near Santa Eulària. All players are welcome and there's a driving range, putting green and comfortable club house. For the less serious golfer, many of the resorts offer mini golf.

Horse Riding

A sunset ride past olive groves and remote *fincas* is a wonderful way to explore the countryside. There are stables at **Sant Antoni**, **Santa Gertrudis**, **Portinatx** and **Santa Eulària**. Most rides are escorted, unless you're very experienced, and the horses are well cared for.

Hunting

Little remains on Ibiza to hunt but local people do shoot partridge and rabbit on weekend forays into the countryside between October and February. If you go for a hike in the country, you'll see rectangular signs, split diagonally into black and white, which designate a hunting area. For those who prefer not to partake in blood sports, clay pigeon shoots take place at weekends.

Tennis

There are few public courts but most large hotels have tennis courts and some, like **Club Med**, will give instruction. Tennis is best restricted to early morning or late afternoon in the peak summer months in order to avoid the heat of the day.

FLAMENCO

Widespread in southern Spain, flamenco is less popular in the Balearics but can be seen at a couple of clubs in Eivissa. Essentially an outlet for passion and unhappiness, good flamenco creates a kind of spiritual bond between musicians, dancer and onlookers as the raw emotion of the song, the hypnotic hand-clapping and finger-snapping of the audience, and the fantastically fast stamping of the dancer build up into a cathartic finale, often accompanied by shouts of encouragement and emotion. Strands of many cultures have come together to form the music as we know it today, but it originates from the 19th-century gypsies of Seville, Jerez and Cadiz who sang laments of lost love and oppression.

RESTAURANTE
EL CORSARIO

2
Eivissa

Centre of both Ibiza's cultural life and social scene, Eivissa is the capital of the island. This beautiful old town is packed with character. The floodlit stone walls of **Dalt Vila**, the 'high town' perched on a steep hill, are visible at night from miles around while below, the bars and clubs of the newer **Sa Marina** district buzz until dawn. Luxury yachts line the harbour at **Botafoch** opposite Dalt Vila and a constant stream of large ferries and container ships give the docks a busy air.

Eivissa is divided into four distinct areas. The imposing walls of Dalt Vila, the fortified medieval section, conceal magnificent old buildings separated by narrow, cobbled streets. Behind Dalt Vila is the hilltop necropolis of **Puig des Molins**, 'hill of the mills', an important Punic burial ground. By far the best way to explore this area is on foot.

In Sa Marina – the area between the walls and the port – a nightly market, pavement cafés, clubs and music bars all jostle for position, with the shuttered, whitewashed buildings slumbering in the heat of the day. The old fishing district of **Sa Penya** juts out into the sea, its crumbling houses teetering precariously close to the cliff edge.

Finally, not considered to be a specific area but forming the rest of the modern town, the **Eixample**, or extension, radiates out around the bay to the Botafoch marina on the opposite side and to the south, where Eivissa blends into the developed resorts of Figueretas and Platja d'en Bossa.

Don't Miss

*** **Dalt Vila:** Eivissa's medieval city.
*** **Archaeological museum:** explore the history of Ibiza and Formentera.
** **Museum of Contemporary Art:** view Spanish and foreign artists.
** **Bar-hopping:** people-watching in the 'Ibiza Triangle'.
* **Montesol:** have coffee at this hotel on Passeig Vara del Rey.

Opposite: *Fortified Dalt Vila rises high above the waterfront of Eivissa town.*

Dalt Vila

A *dalt vila* is not unique to Ibiza; most old Mediterranean towns are divided into upper and lower areas. The streets around the port were where working class people and fishermen would live, while noblemen and those holding religious positions would remain in the fortified safety of the upper town, away from pirate attacks. Ironically, it is now the wealthy who frequent the port of Eivissa and the elderly who live in the narrow streets of Dalt Vila.

Dalt Vila ★★★

Dalt Vila is a must for any visitor to Ibiza. Explore the old town early in the morning, when the permanent residents are up and about and the visitors are still sleeping off the excesses of the night before. Alternatively, sunset gives the yellow sandstone walls a warm glow and the streets are virtually deserted as the coach parties head back to their hotels. Old ladies in black sit outside their houses, dogs and cats bask in the last heat of the day, and the occasional television blares from a cool, dark living room.

The narrow streets form an absolute maze, some linked by ancient steps and some reaching dead ends. Without a map, simply head upwards to reach all the important monuments, including the cathedral and the castle, and down to get back to Sa Marina. Surprising views keep appearing through buildings or round corners as dazzling sunlight reflects off the whitewashed structures and the Mediterranean glitters below.

Opposite: *A lengthy Latin inscription to King Philip II crowns the Portal de Ses Taules.*

Walking around Dalt Vila

The 'high town' is actually divided into various fortified sections. Archaeologists believe that the very highest point, where the cathedral stands today, has been a place of worship for over 2500 years and was used first as the site for a Phoenician temple. This area was the original Dalt Vila, although the term now refers to everything within the walls. The cathedral, the castle and the citadel were enclosed by walls during medieval times; later fortifications took place in 1554, during which time the bastions were constructed.

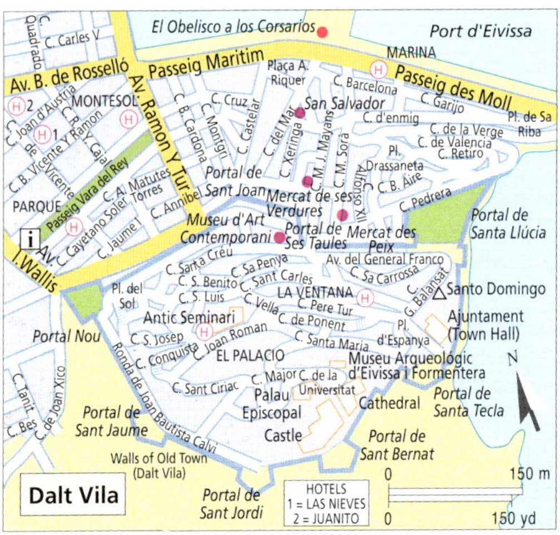

Today, the layout of

the town appears chaotic, as is common with medieval town planning – when places expanded simply according to their defensive needs. Below the original Dalt Vila, still within the walls, is the old **Vila Mitjana** (the 'middle town') and below that, **Vila d'Avall** (the 'lower town'), where the poor would have lived. The area to the east, around the Ajuntament (Town Hall), is the **Vila Nova**, or 'new town', a mere 400 years old.

The Walls ***

Eivissa's sand-coloured city walls are classified as a National Monument and represent one of the best preserved military fortifications in Europe. In 1554 King Carlos I commissioned the Italian architect **Calvi** to fortify the city against the increasing number of raids from marauding Turks. The construction was carried out by Pere Francés and Gaspar Puig and supervised by the French architect Jacob Fratin. Calvi, the designer, was also responsible for the bulwarks of the shipyards in Barcelona and part of the walls around Palma in neighbouring Mallorca.

The seemingly impenetrable Renaissance walls are accessed by three gates: the Portal de Ses Taules (completed 40 years after the original fortification of the city), the **Portal Nou** and the **Portal de Sant Joan**. Huge bulwarks around the exterior also allow access through solid wooden gates. The **Portal de Ses Taules** is actually located inside the original Renaissance walls to guard the central citadel from attack. The approach is startling: one minute you're wandering past the shops and cafés of the Sa Marina district and the next, a towering gate and stone ramp loom up ahead. A stone coat of arms adorns the gate accompanied by a long Latin inscription paying homage to King Philip II, during

Carthaginian Beliefs

The Carthaginians lived in what is now Dalt Vila and worshipped a number of gods, including **Melkart**, the protector of sailors. Melkart was served by priests, who remained celibate, dressed in linen and went everywhere barefoot. Women and pigs were not allowed in the temple, where a sacred fire was kept burning.

Ibiza's red soil was believed to have magical properties and even those living in Carthage in North Africa wished to spend their last days here.

In the 6th century BC, the Carthaginians stopped cremating their dead and began to bury them, further reinforcing their belief in an afterlife. Egyptian-style amulets were buried with the dead as symbols of resurrection.

Legend of the Reconquest

Legend has it that the Catalan-Aragon army led by Jaume I in 1235 was able to enter the city because of the absent-mindedness of the town's Muslim governor. His brother, a sheik, had allegedly fallen in love with a slave girl in the harem of the governor and had abducted her. The governor was so distressed that he failed to notice the arrival of Jaume I's troops, who stormed the city. There was certainly a gateway at the spot where a commemorative chapel is located in Carrer Sant Ciriac, but no one knows whether the romantic story is true or whether in fact the governor opened the door to Jaume I's troops to attempt peaceful negotiation.

whose reign the walls were completed in 1585. Headless statues in white marble, reproductions of Roman pieces almost certainly unearthed during the 16th-century construction of the walls, stand on either side.

Today, it is possible to walk around most of the solid ramparts, trying to envisage how it must have felt when Turkish enemy sails appeared over the shimmering horizon. There are several vantage points from which the inhabitants of the city would have thrown missiles from the ramparts onto the heads of the approaching enemy.

Immediately inside the Portal de Ses Taules is the **Plaça de Vila**, a street lined with outdoor restaurants, chic art galleries and souvenir shops. Evenings in summer are the best time to catch the atmosphere here as residents of the area enjoy a *passeig* before settling down for supper under the stars.

Museu d'Art Contemporani **

Immediately to the left of the main gate is the Museum of Contemporary Art. Upstairs there's a changing exhibition by Spanish and foreign artists, while a permanent display of oils is located in the lower part of the building. The views from the balcony looking down over the town

Right: *An exhibition of local and foreign artists in the Museu d'Art Contemporani changes every two months.*

from the eastern ramparts are breathtaking. Open 10:00–13:30 and 17:00–20:00 April to September; 10:00–14:00 in winter; closed Monday.

From here, make your way upwards through the narrow streets towards the looming mass of the cathedral. At the end of Carrer Sa Carrossa there are stunning views from the **Baluard de Santa Llúcia** across the harbour to the hills beyond and towards the saltpans of the far south. Up a flight of steps from the ramparts is the pleasant **Plaça d'Espanya**, site of the **Ajuntament** (Town Hall) which was built originally in the 17th century as a Dominican convent. Concerts and recitals are held occasionally in the small chapel here, but the Town Hall is not open to casual visitors.

Santo Domingo ★

Before you reach the cathedral, pay a visit to the red-roofed church of Santo Domingo, a building that looks as though it belongs on a Greek island with its tiled domes and dazzling white walls. The frescoes on the vault were created by two brothers who lived on the island during the 19th century.

Above: *Centrepiece of Plaça d'Espanya is this statue dedicated by the Ajuntament to 'people of the sea'.*

Early Influences

Many aspects of life in these islands were introduced by their various conquerors. In the 7th century BC the Carthaginians brought new building techniques, a system of writing, iron metallurgy, chickens, vines, olive trees and pottery kilns, while the Moors later introduced citrus trees, peaches, pepper, cinnamon, coriander and cumin. Much later still, the islands shared in the spoils from the New World, which included tomatoes, maize, potatoes and, of course, tobacco.

Above: *A Roman temple is believed to have once occupied the site of Eivissa's cathedral.*

The Cathedral ★★

Ibiza's amber-coloured cathedral, high up on the hill of Dalt Vila, is the largest church on the island and is dedicated to the Virgin Mary – in this case, **Santa Maria de las Neus**, or Mary of the Snows, a peculiarity for an island that hardly ever sees snow. Construction was begun in the 14th century and completed in the 16th; the original building would have been Catalan Gothic in style.

Later modifications to the city walls meant that the cathedral's shape was changed and the only original Gothic features that remain are the bell tower and the vestry. The remainder is in rather sombre, plain baroque style, although there are several stunning silver altarpieces inside from the 14th and 15th centuries, as well as some early Gothic paintings and the tombs of various eminent Ibizenco families. Under the walls, the remains of an Arabic mosque have been discovered and there are signs that a Roman temple once stood on this site. Open 10:00–19:00 every day except Monday, 10:00–16:00 in winter.

Museu Arqueológic d'Eivissa i Formentera ★★★

Opposite the cathedral, the beautifully laid out archaeological museum is housed in a pretty, sand-coloured Gothic chapel that was once the home of the **Universitat** – not a seat of learning but the governing body of Ibiza after the Catalan conquest of the 13th century. After the war of succession to the Spanish Crown in the 18th century, the Universitat was downgraded to a city council and eventually moved to different premises in the Dominican Convent, where it still stands today.

The museum is compact at ground level but spreads over several storeys inside the 16th-century bulwark of **Santa Tecla**. Its exhibits chart the island's history from prehistoric times to the Islamic period. Artefacts are

Punic Cuisine

The Carthaginians and the Romans had a strong influence on Ibiza's cuisine, and dishes dating from this period can still be sampled on the island. Typical items would have been asparagus, almond sauce, fish with the pungent *garum* paste, and game birds like pigeon and partridge with figs or dates.

housed in long stone corridors or in cool, white-walled rooms with vaulted ceilings, and range from ancient coins to statuettes and beautiful glassware.

Prehistoric and Bronze Ages: Relatively little is known about Ibiza before the Bronze Age. In the Bronze Age people lived in caves and in communities located on higher ground, and there are remains of defensive structures at Sa Cala and Punta des Jondal on Ibiza, suggesting tension between these communities. Metal objects indicate some kind of foreign trade, as there are no ores of that kind on Ibiza. Items on display include simple pottery objects; a few personal ornaments such as buttons and beads made from pig tusk, bone and shell (found in the megalithic tomb of Ca Na Costa on Formentera); and pestles and mortars. There are also some cutting tools made from flint and bone.

Between 1000 and 650BC it is known that tools were moulded at workshops in Mallorca and Menorca. Concentrations of these have been found on Formentera and at a few coastal sites around Ibiza; a variety of axes is on display in the museum.

Phoenician Settlement: Active trade with other areas of the Mediterranean began during the second half of the 7th century BC when Phoenicians colonized Ibiza. Finds from this era are more elaborate than previous discoveries and include both hand-modelled pottery – usually pots used for cooking – and wheel-turned items like storage jars and amphorae, some of which come from the central Mediterranean area. The biggest concentration of these items was found at Sa Caleta on the island's south coast, where there was a large Phoenician settlement before Eivissa became the heart of activity. Fishing, bread baking, weaving and metallurgy were all everyday activities and exhibits include copper and iron knives, fish hooks and weights for weaving looms.

Scorpio Island

Occultists believe that Ibiza's magical powers stem from the fact that the island is governed by the sign of Scorpio, a sign of extremes, of destruction and regeneration. Throughout history strange cults, witchcraft and UFO sightings have been reported on Ibiza. Because the island is believed to have regenerative powers, Carthaginians wanted to be buried here and their ostrich eggs, a symbol of resurrection, can be seen in the archaeological museum. In the 1950s, Ibiza had the highest suicide rate in Spain, again attributed to Scorpio's destructive side.

Below: *Deceptively large and beautifully laid out, the archaeological museum holds important finds, including Punic terracottas.*

TRADITIONAL COSTUMES

Like the dances, local costumes are strikingly original. Men wear red hats, bandannas, gold-trimmed black jackets, and loose fitting white shirts and trousers with a scarlet cummerbund. The women's costumes are more ornate – a long, pleated black or white skirt, silk shawl and a brilliantly coloured embroidered apron. A lacy scarf covers the hair, and the whole outfit is adorned with heavy and elaborate gold jewellery – necklaces, crucifixes, heavy rings and an intricate *emprendad* – a necklace made of gold filigree dating back to Moorish times.

Plates, bowls, amphorae and patterned jars have been found in the **Puig des Molins** site outside Eivissa, along with ornate imports including scarabs from Egypt bearing hieroglyphics, phials for perfumed oil and oil burners.

Punic Times: Indications of early religion have been found at numerous sites in the form of amulets and terracottas (small pottery objects bearing images of the various gods that were worshipped). At the site of Illa Plana in Eivissa, which was excavated in 1907, clay figures with clearly defined sexual organs were discovered, indicating the presence of fertility rituals. In the cave of Es Cuieram, near Sant Vicent in the north of the island, hundreds of clay images of the goddess Tanit were discovered.

Also on display from this era are glazed wheel-turned pots, copies from other areas of the Mediterranean. Tableware is modelled on the Greek style and covered with a grey paste.

As Ibiza flourished, its first mint was opened, and in the 3rd century BC coins were made bearing the image of the god Bes. Most are bronze but some are made of silver. Coins from Rome, also of bronze and silver, have been found and date from around the 3rd century BC.

Below: *Ornate jewellery and a bright apron are part of the women's traditional costume.*

During Punic times, many things were imported, particularly luxury items such as glass beads, necklaces and jewels. The ostrich egg on display in the museum was found in the necropolis at Puig des Molins, and is believed to have been buried as a symbol of resurrection.

Roman Empire: Three Roman statues, probably once destined for a square or public place, are exhibited in the museum. It is believed that the statues were found during the construction of the Renaissance walls of the city in 1555, as they were used to decorate the completed walls in 1585. In 1980, however, they were replaced by replicas and the originals moved to the museum and restored.

Other interesting finds from Roman times include quality pieces of glass, mostly pots that would have held unguents and oils used for burning in lamps and as perfumes.

As the Romans focused production on the parts of their empire that had the best resources, Ibiza's output gradually declined during the 1st century AD. Amphorae dated around this era would have probably contained imports like Italian wine and salted fish from mainland Spain.

Above: *Modified sporadically over the centuries, the castle displays a curious mixture of architectural styles.*

Islamic Times: A lot of gold and silver coins with Islamic inscriptions have been dated between the 7th and 12th centuries, from mints in Palma on nearby Mallorca, Córdoba and Seville on the Spanish mainland, and Fez in Morocco. Glass pots have been traced to Persia and Egypt but pots and flasks were made locally using clay from the mainland.

A visit to the museum is a must, and provides a valuable aid to gaining an understanding of the history of Ibiza and Formentera before travelling around the islands. Open 10:00–13:00, 16:00–19:00. Closed Monday.

The Castle **

Continue towards the entrance **Es Soto Fosc** in the rampart, from which there are more stunning views, this time to the south. On a clear day you can easily see across to the island of Formentera.

After admiring the scenery, head down the narrow street of **Carrer de la Universitat** between the castle and the cathedral towards the entrance to the castle. A flight of steps leads off this narrow street. On the first landing there is an opening cut into the rock, believed to be a cistern dating back to the Phoenician period over 2500 years ago – the staircase was only completed in 1993.

The **castle** (*castell*) itself is a mishmash of architectural styles, the original keep having been constructed by the Arabs and final touches still being added as recently as

Sherry Drinking

Fino is a national institution in Spain and although it is produced in Andalucía in the south, it is drunk everywhere as an aperitif. In addition to *fino*, two other types of sherry are drunk throughout Spain. *Manzanilla* is a type of dry fino with a salty tang, making a perfect accompaniment to seafood. *Amontillado*, meanwhile, is a considerably more pungent wine that has been aged beyond its normal span in the *bodega*, while *olloroso*, the heaviest style of sherry, is usually sweetened and sold as 'cream' exclusively to the British market.

the 18th century. The towers that flank the main entrance were once part of the town's medieval walls. There are plans to convert the castle into a luxury hotel, although local people are sceptical that this will ever happen. The castle is currently not open to visitors.

Carrer Major ★

Walk from the castle down the Carrer Major and admire the old noblemen's houses, dating back to the 15th century. Several are still adorned by a family coat of arms.

Number one, built in the 15th century, has a Gothic appearance and is called **Can Bardaixi–Can Clara**, meaning 'the house of Bardaixi and Clara'. Numbers three to six were built later, in the 18th century, while number seven was once the administrative building for the saltpans in the island's far south.

Tiny streets lead off the Carrer Major; take a quick detour down **Sa Portella**, a tiny gateway leading to Carrer Santa Maria. At the end is **Can Balansat**, a well-preserved house with the original 17th-century windows still intact.

Back on Carrer Major, number 14 was a chapel in the 16th century, while number 18, **Can Llaudis**, is a beautiful old Catalan Gothic home which is being converted into a museum to house work by the Puget painters. A father-and-son team, the Pugets are considered to be the best known of Ibiza's impressionist painters.

Where Carrer Major becomes **Carrer Sant Ciriac**, a tiny chapel built in 1754 marks the point where a special

ANIS

Aniseed-flavoured drinks are very popular on Ibiza and Formentera and two types are produced locally on a small scale, either to be made into *hierbas* or as drinks in their own right. *Anís dulce* is sweet, while *anís seco* is dry. Visitors prefer to dilute the potent brew with water – as one would with Greek ouzo or French pastis – but locals drink it straight up. One type, *palo*, is dark brown in colour and requires a lot of ice to make it palatable.

Mass is held annually to celebrate the reconquest of the city by Jaume I from the Moors. Take a sharp right into **Carrer Joan Roman**, leading back towards the cathedral, and you will pass the **Antic Seminari** on the left, one of the last remaining buildings from Moorish times. There's a wonderful restaurant up a narrow flight of steps to the right, **El Corsario**, ideal for a much deserved drink on the shady terrace which looks out over the whole of Eivissa town. The restaurant is situated in the former mansion of a corsair, hence its name.

Pa Amb Aioli

Inevitably in an Ibizenco restaurant, bread with garlic mayonnaise is brought to the table. The mayonnaise is a speciality of nearby Menorca and is named after Maó, the capital, where it was first invented over a century ago. The recipe combines olive oil, egg yolks and a touch of lemon juice, possibly a little freshly ground black pepper and sea-salt, garlic or fresh herbs to flavour. The Ibizenco version is powerfully laced with garlic, so beware! (Chewing fresh parsley is supposed to be an antidote to garlic breath.)

Nights in Dalt Vila

The old town is popular with gays, many of whom stay in the nearby resort of Figueretas. There's an easy-going, lively atmosphere after dark and lots of bars to explore. Shops stay open until after 22:00 in the peak season.

Just inside the medieval walls, the street **Sa Carrossa** is lined with bars, many of them catering to a gay clientele, while to the right (looking up the hill) of Portal de Ses Taules, the more mainstream **Plaça de Vila** is an attractive street that's home to numerous bars and rather elegant restaurants with outdoor seating.

There are a few tiny hotels in Dalt Vila, all carefully hidden from the masses with the notable exception of **El Palacio** which declares itself to be the 'Hotel of the Movie Stars' and adorns its outside walls with handprints of the famous. Opposite, the tiny **Bar La Cueva** has outdoor chairs and strange sculptures inside its welcoming gloom.

Opposite: *Dalt Vila's higgledy-piggledy streets are lined with enticing restaurants.*
Below: *Stone motifs adorn the entrance to many a home in Dalt Vila.*

Noblemen's Houses ★

Outside the walls of Dalt Vila, there are plenty more interesting streets through which to wander. **Carrer Bisbe Torres**, the street leading up to the Portal de Ses Taules, has a number of beautiful old houses with arched doorways and intricate iron balconies which once belonged to the aristocrats of the city, among them merchants, landowners and wealthy seamen. Look for the coat of arms above the door, usually engraved into the amber stone.

OLIVES

Olives were introduced to Ibiza by the Carthaginians who grafted special varieties on to wild trees. Olives are, in fact, grown and served all over Spain as a form of tapas although the best are said to come from the south, both because of the superior fruit yielded by the trees there and the special dressing which gives the olives their unique flavour. Cumin seeds, wild marjoram, rosemary, thyme, bay leaf, garlic, savoury and fennel are all used in a recipe handed down from Moorish times. Several types of olive are served as tapas throughout Spain: *aceituna de la reina*, the Queen's olive and the most prized; *aceituna gorda*, the 'fat olive'; *manzanilla*, a fine, dry flavoured fruit; and the black olive.

SA PENYA ★

Much of Eivissa lies on reclaimed land but Sa Penya, the old fishermen's district, is genuine. Clinging to a tiny spur of rock jutting out into the harbour below Dalt Vila, the ancient houses look as though they are about to tumble into the water.

Sa Penya used to be a busy little suburb of Eivissa located next to **Sa Dracaneta**, the former shipyard, and **Sa Bomba**, the port. Today's inhabitants, however, are poor working-class people and gypsies. The tiny streets have plenty of atmosphere, with washing strung overhead between the houses and draped over the peeling paintwork. The houses look as though they were built to accommodate the uneven rocky surface of the peninsula and years of battering by winds from the sea have left buildings further distorted, their staircases crooked and twisted.

Old people gossip in doorways or sit outside in the shade, watching the world go by. Not many visitors choose to explore this faded labyrinth, and most people prefer to photograph the old façades and twisted balconies from the water, on the decks of the Formentera-bound ferries.

Bars To Be Seen In

These are some of the island's most trendy bars, cafés and restaurants:
Sunset Cafe and **Barzuka** in Eivissa;
Jazz Club in Eivissa;
Indiana Café, at the 5km marker on the Eivissa–Sant Antoni road;
DC10, quirky bar en route to Ses Salines;
Café del Mar and **Kumharas** in Sant Antoni;
Malibu in Ses Salines: beach bar for beautiful people;
Base and **The Rock** in Eivissa for people-watching.

Above: *Eivissa's restaurants are full of atmosphere during summer.*
Below: *The tip of the Sa Penya district clings precariously to the rock.*

Sa Marina ★★★

Sa Marina, everybody's first impression of Eivissa town, is sleepy and deserted by day and hopping with life after dark. This is the area located between the dockside and the walls of Dalt Vila, bordered by Sa Penya and the Eixample. In this warren of narrow alleys, visitors spend time shopping, eating, drinking, parading and browsing between sunset and midnight when the clubs open.

An easy landmark for the entrance to the '**Ibiza Triangle**' – the hub of all the nightlife – is **El Obelisco a los Corsarios** (Obelisk of the Corsairs), a monument to Ibiza's privateers which stands on the dock. The corsarios, or corsairs, were local heroes, protecting the island against Barbary pirates for hundreds of years. If you turn away from the port at this point, you will find yourself in the very heart of the Triangle, with numerous trendy bars all thudding out music at top volume. Cocktails here are spectacular but very expensive and obtaining a seat outside is equivalent to sitting in the front row of the stalls for watching the parade of weird and wonderful people passing by.

Deeper into the narrow streets is a kind of posh hippie market with stalls selling jewellery, clubbing gear, paintings, pottery,

Right: *Sa Marina leads to the waterfront, its streets more regular than Dalt Vila.*

TIPPING

A service charge is always included in hotel bills and sometimes in restaurant bills. Where it is not included, 10% of the total is an appropriate tip. Taxi drivers and bartenders will also be happy with around 10%. Many filling stations are not self service, in which case you should tip the attendant up to 100 pesetas. The same applies to hotel porters. Generally, though, the attitude to tipping is more relaxed than in the USA, for example, and some taxi drivers have even been known to decline a tip.

straw baskets, wood carvings, wind chimes and, of course, the famous Ibiza Ad Lib fashions. Shops stretch back into the cave-like cellars, displaying tie-dye dresses, wafty white numbers for the clubs and trademark white lace and floaty cotton garments.

Streets that are not crammed with market stalls are a mass of restaurants, most fairly uninspiring for the gourmet but buzzing with atmosphere on a summer night. Real foodies should stay off the beaten track but for a good pizza, this is the place. Afterwards, there are jazz and rock bars, coffee shops and pubs to explore before the nightclubs open at midnight.

COFFEE

Good, strong espresso-style coffee is normally drunk in Spain but there are plenty of alternatives. *Cafe con leche* is made with hot milk, while cappuccino is frothy. *Cafe cortado* is espresso with cold milk and *cafe solo* is black coffee. Nescafé invariably means a sachet of decaffeinated. Liqueur coffees are often drunk after meals (and occasionally with breakfast).

Markets ★

There are two markets in the Sa Marina district between the walls of Dalt Vila and the port, both providing plenty of local colour. One is the **Mercat des Peix**, the old fish market. The octagonal building has an unusual drainage system on the roof which channels all the water to one side. Early morning is the best time to visit.

Eivissa's other market, **Mercat de ses Verdures** (the vegetable market) is located in the Plaça de la Constitució, a colourful scene in a rather bizarre neoclassical building. As with the fish market, it is best to visit this early in the morning.

Eixample and around the Bay

Passeig Vara del Rey ★★★

This astonishingly beautiful street is the hub of Eivissa's Eixample, or 'new section', and is located a couple of blocks back from the harbour. Benches line the shady central section and the façades of the elegant, 19th-century buildings are beautifully preserved, particularly the **Hotel Montesol** which was built in the 1930s and which is today one of Eivissa's most distinguished coffee houses. Outside, the walls are painted in ochre and white while smart wooden shutters give the building an atmospheric feel. Ceiling fans whir silently inside and coffee drinkers gather to people-watch and read the morning papers.

The statue at the centre of the *passeig* is of **General Joaquim Vara del Rey** (1840–89), an Ibizenco soldier who died in the Battle of Caney in Cuba, defending his country against the United States Army. The neoclassical sculpture of the hero surrounded by winged angels was created in 1904 by the sculptors Alentorce and Font Carreras and was unveiled by King Alfonso XIII.

Above: *Straw baskets for sale in Eivissa's upmarket equivalent of a hippie market.*

Below: *Numerous stalls make for great leisurely browsing.*

Elsewhere in the street are sundry cafés, shops, news kiosks and a branch of the tourist office. The large bookshop on the right-hand side sells a selection of English language newspapers.

Should you be here during August, be sure to visit this street for the nonstop entertainment. Between the 5th and the 8th of August in particular, the tree-lined central area is packed with musicians, dancers, entertainers and merrymaking in celebration of the town's main festival.

Plaça de Toros *

Just inland from the port is Ibiza's unremarkable bullring, attracting minor-league matadors and bulls but nonetheless offering an evening out for those interested in something inherently Spanish. The really big fights, in which the matadors are millionaires and the bulls are from the country's finest bloodstock farms, take place on the mainland in Madrid, Barcelona and Seville, but Ibiza's bullring does have its following.

ADDRESSES IN IBIZA

Often, an address in Spain is expressed by its position on the road according to the kilometre markers, rather than the street number. For example, Privilege nightclub's address is Carretera Eivissa-Sant Antoni km7. This makes places easy to find, particularly on country roads. The address is simply translated to mean that the nightclub is located on the road from Eivissa to Sant Antoni at the 7km road marker. All main roads in Spain and many country lanes have marker stones every kilometre, and the system is used for houses, hotels and office buildings.

Be warned, however, that the bull is always killed in a Spanish bullfight and some visitors may find the spectacle gory. There is little point in taking a high moral stand at a *corrida*; bullfighting plays a deep-seated role in Spanish history and attracts a huge audience. Classified as an art rather than a sport, it is an event of great skill and bravery (on the part of both bull and matador) and the costumes are spectacular. If you are opposed to bullfighting, simply don't attend.

Casino *

Close to **Pacha**, the island's most exclusive nightclub, located on the Botafoch side of the marina on **Passeig Maritim**, is Ibiza's casino. The establishment is open all year round. Roulette, blackjack and craps are available and the stakes are fairly low – all you need is a passport or ID to enter. Earlier on during the evening the casino is packed with tourists, with the serious gamblers arriving in the small hours to patronize the private gaming rooms.

The casino complex also has a nightclub with a cabaret show, and a restaurant serving a mixture of Spanish and international cuisine.

Opposite top: *The Hotel Montesol was built in the 1930s and houses a distinguished coffee house.*
Opposite bottom: *Passeig Vara del Rey becomes a focal point of the town during festivals.*
Below: *The island's only casino draws gamblers all year round.*

Reading the Map

The half-way transition from Castilian Spanish to Catalan, or Eivissenc, can be confusing to visitors. Some street signs have been changed and some left, while maps often have a mixture of *playa* and *platja* for beach, and *carrer* and *calle* for street. A *cala* is Catalan for a cove or fjord, while a *cova*, confusingly, is a cave. *Puig* or *serra* means hill and, in towns, *avinguda* is the Catalan for *avenida*, or avenue. In either language, if the address of a house is s/n, it means 'no number', while the abbreviation *aptdo* is similar to a box number.

South of Town

Puig des Molins ★★★

Just behind Dalt Vila is a steep hill topped with several windmills which have given rise to the name 'Hill of Mills'. The area of Puig des Molins, now protected, contains an important Carthaginian and Roman necropolis with over 3000 tombs excavated from the rock like giant molehills. The necropolis was used for almost 1000 years, from the 7th century BC to the 3rd century AD, and countless treasures have been retrieved from its tombs.

Breakfast

Breakfast is not a big event in Spain, although restaurants all over Ibiza and Formentera offer a traditional English fry-up. A typical local breakfast would include coffee, tea or hot chocolate with pastries, or bread with jam or honey. *Ensaimadas*, a local speciality, are sweet rolls made with lard, while *churros* are sweet doughnuts to dip in hot chocolate. Don't be shocked to see workers in a café consuming a beer with their coffee – it's quite common!

Figueretas ★

Beyond Puig des Molins, Eivissa has spread into one long development stretching south along the sweep of **Platja d'en Bossa**. The northern end of this beach forms the resort of **Figueretas**, slightly more refined than its neighbours, with some smart hotels and a cosmopolitan atmosphere which attracts a lot of gay visitors.

Platja d'en Bossa ★

A long, thin ribbon of hotels and apartments, Platja d'en Bossa is popular with families because of its gently shelving beach. There are plenty of facilities here ranging from water-skiing and windsurfing schools to lively bars and restaurants. One family favourite is the

Aguamar water park (open summer only), a wet and wild experience of water slides including the Curly Wurly, a dizzying spiral, as its name implies, and Kamikaze, 16m (52ft) of terrifying free fall. Two bars and restaurants and a picnic area mean you can make a day of the park and a re-entry pass allows visitors to leave and explore Platja d'en Bossa for a while.

Platja d'en Bossa is an ideal location for night owls with easy access to the bars and clubs of Eivissa. The resort is also famous for **Space**, one of the island's most legendary clubs, which opens at 06:00! Die-hard ravers flock to Space to chill out after a night of excess and slowly pick their way to the warm sand to sleep at midday when the club closes.

Those in pursuit of a healthier lifestyle will enjoy the easy if lengthy walk from Bossa to **Platja de Migjorn**, the long, remote stretch of sand in the island's deep south. A roughly hewn coastal path is marked with occasional red dots painted on the stones. You'll need good, strong shoes as the path twists and turns over scenery varying from soft dunes to jagged volcanic rock, but the gradients are easy and the scenery beautiful once the path has left the busy resort.

Opposite: *Bereft of its sail, a windmill tower stands disused on Puig des Molins.*
Below: *Platja d'en Bossa's gently shelving beach is ideal for families.*

Eivissa at a Glance

Best Times to Visit

The town is lively year-round but with a very pronounced tourist season from **early May** until **late October**. Many bars and restaurants shut down for the rest of the year. In May, many of the nightclubs have opening parties which are worth attending. **July** and **August** are packed months, when the nightlife is at its best. The climate is pleasant but the summer months are very hot and less appropriate for sightseeing.

Local saints' days:
Nit de Sant Joan, 23 June;
Santa Maria, 5 August;
Sant Ciriac, 8 August.

Getting There

The **airport** is just 10 minutes' drive from Eivissa, and is served by buses and taxis. **Ferries** sail regularly between Eivissa town, the island's main port, and Formentera, as well as the other Balearic islands and the Spanish mainland.

Airport Information, tel: 971 30 12 54.

Shipping companies:
Trasmediterranea, tel: 971 31 50 50;
Flebasa, tel: 971 34 28 71.

Getting Around

The choice is between public bus, hired car, motorbike, bicycle or taxi. **Public buses** are cheap and efficient and run to a regular schedule from Eivissa to Sant Antoni and Santa Eulària, which between them constitute the two main arterial routes on the island. Local buses to more remote villages run from these two resorts.

Cars, **motorbikes** and **bicycles** can all be rented for reasonable rates in Eivissa. Try Tony Rent for all three, e-mail: telapes@teledire.es tel: 971 30 08 79. **Roads** are good and driving reasonably sedate, although Spanish drivers have a habit of driving very close to the car in front if they think it's travelling too slowly. Driving is on the right. Off the main roads, many of the most scenic routes are via dirt track, so it is advisable to hire a **mountain bike** for more adventurous exploration.

There are **taxi ranks** in Passeig Vara del Rey and Figueretas

Bus companies:
website: www.ibizabus.com
The Discobus operates at night between Eivissa and Sant Antoni, tel: 971 19 24 56.

Where to Stay

The beach resorts of **Talamanca**, **Platja d'en Bossa** and **Figueretas** get very busy in summer with package tour business, so book well ahead. Accommodation in **Eivissa** itself is also hard to come by, most visitors preferring to stay on the beach.

Stay in **Dalt Vila** for best access to nightlife and, paradoxically, a taste of Ibizenco lifestyle.

Luxury

La Ventana, Plaça Sa Carrossa 13, 07800 Eivissa, tel: 971 30 35 37, fax: 971 39 01 45. Elegant, stylish hotel in Dalt Vila with stunning views. Traditional island-style with some modern touches. Open all year-round.

Hotel El Palacio, Carrer de la Conquista 2, tel: 971 30 14 78, fax: 971 39 15 81. Smart hideaway in lovely setting in Dalt Vila with just seven suites. Frequented by celebrities.

La Torre del Canonigo, Carrer Mayor 8, tel: 971 30 38 84, fax: 971 30 78 43. Fabulous views from a 14th century tower.

Mid-range

El Corsario, Carrer Poniente 5, Dalt Vila, tel: 971 30 14 04, fax: 971 39 19 53. Two-star *hostal* in Dalt Vila in converted old mansion. Eccentric and charming rather than luxurious. Closed winter.

Hostal Residence Rocamar, Talamanca, Eivissa, tel: 971 31 79 22, fax: 971 31 78 22. New *hostal* close to Talamanca beach on the opposite side of the bay from Eivissa.

Hotel Torre del Mar, Platja Den Bossa, Eivissa, tel: 971 30 30 50, fax: 971 30 40 60. Four-star hotel with pool and good facilities.

Eivissa at a Glance

Hotel Los Molinos, Ramon Muntaner 60, Eivissa, tel: 971 30 22 50, fax: 971 30 25 04. Situated in centre of modern part of town.

Budget

Hotel Montesol, Passeig Vara del Rey, Eivissa, tel: 971 31 01 61. Beautiful colonial-style building facing the port. Famous coffee shop on ground floor.

Where to Eat

There are plenty of restaurants around the port, in the streets below the walls of Dalt Vila, and along the beaches of Talamanca, Figueretas and Platja d'en Bossa. The following have character and serve homemade specialities.

Meson de Paco, Carrer Bartolome Rosello, Eivissa, tel: 971 31 42 24. Local specialities in one of Eivissa's oldest restaurants. Open year-round, closed Wednesdays.

Ca N'Alfredo, Passeig Vara del Rey 16, tel: 971 31 12 74. Open for nearly 70 years; serves traditional island dishes.

Restaurante Principe, Edificio Principe, Platja de Figueretas, tel: 971 30 19 14. Seafood and fish specialities on the beach in Figueretas.

El Faro, Plaça Garijo, Sa Penya, tel: 971 31 32 33. Atmospheric restaurant in old fishing quarter of Sa Penya. Seafood specialities served on large terrace.

Michelangelo, Marina Botafoch, tel: 971 19 04 67. Homemade pasta and Italian specialities in elegant setting, overlooking Botafoch marina.

La Brasa, Pere Sala, Eivissa, tel: 971 30 12 02. Unusual local specialities served in pretty garden just below walls of Dalt Vila. Try salmon with lobster sauce or duck with plums.

El Olivo, Plaça de Vila 8, Dalt Vila, tel: 971 30 06 80. Superb fish and local specialities in prime people-watching position. Good wine list.

The Dome, Carrer d' Alfonso X11. Local dishes in palm-shaded courtyard.

Nightlife

Pacha, Passeig Perimetral (on the port at Botafoch), tel: 971 31 36 00. Exclusive and popular. Open daily from May, weekends only in winter, www.pacha.com

El Divino, Puerto de Eivissa Nueva. Busy and popular gay club, tel: 971 19 01 76. www.eldivino-ibiza.com

Angels, Passeig de Juan Carlos s/n.

Space, Platja d'en Bossa. Legendary club, hard core techno/rave, open 06:00 until midday, tel: 971 39 67 95.

Anfora, Carrer Sant Carlos 7, Dalt Vila.

Shopping

Shops, boutiques and a nightly hippie market are concentrated in the **Sa Marina** district as well as two food markets, one specializing in fish, the other in vegetables. Art galleries are mainly located in Dalt Vila.

Tours and Excursions

Ferries run regularly to Formentera from the dockside at intervals ranging from one an hour in winter to one every 15 minutes during summer.

Coach excursions can be booked for round-the-island tours, as well as trips to the hippie market in **Es Canar** and up to the remote north of Ibiza. Small **boats** run from the port to all the beaches along the east coast for reasonable fees. Alternatively, **charter** a **speedboat** or a **yacht** from one of the outlets at the marina.

Water Park: Aguamar at Playa d' en Bossa is open daily, 10:00–19:00, tel: 971 396 790.

Boat charter: Cruiser Ibiza, Puerto Deportivo Marina Botafoch, tel: 971 31 61 70.

Coral Yachting, address as above, tel: 971 31 39 26.

Keywest, address as above, tel: 971 31 60 70.

Organized tours: Barceló Viatges, Avinguda San José s/n, 07800 Eivissa, tel: 971 30 12 54.

Viatges Urbis, Avinguda d'Agost s/n, Edificia Brisol 07800, Eivissa, tel: 971 31 44 12.

Useful Contacts

Police, Carrer Vicente Serra 25, tel: 971 31 58 61.

Tourist office, Av. Anderes, tel: 971 30 19 00.

3
Sant Antoni and Surrounds

Along way from Eivissa in style, big brash Sant Antoni is the heart of the island's package tour industry. From a distance, and with a little imagination, the town looks like a part of Rio de Janeiro, a magnificent sweep of blue bay lined with blindingly white skyscrapers and inviting sandy beaches, culminating in a steep headland.

Close up, the town is young, exuberant and fun-loving, packed with entertainment day and night, its beaches lined with bronzed bodies. Sant Antoni, or **San An**, as visitors soon learn to call it, is a good base from which to explore Ibiza's west coast. The town itself is divided into the **West End**, where all the best nightlife takes place, and the **Bay**, a massive semicircle of development stretching several kilometres out from the town. At night, its lights reflect off the water, forming pools of colour. Around the rocky headlands to the north and south are strings of exquisite bays, some accessible only by boat, with perfect white sand, rocks from which to snorkel and perhaps a tiny beach bar. **Cala Bassa**, **Cala Conta** and **Cala Tarida** are all stunning and relatively uncrowded in high season. In addition there are wonderful walks along the cliffs.

Sant Antoni is only 15km (9½ miles) from Eivissa and bus services between the two are frequent. At night, special buses run to the village of **Sant Rafel** in the centre of the island where two of the most famous clubs, **Privilege** and **Amnesia,** are based. For many young people these clubs are the prime reason for visiting Ibiza.

DON'T MISS

*** **Boat trips:** particularly to the remote *calas* around the coast.
*** **A visit to Privilege:** one of Europe's most spectacular nightclubs.
** **Ceramics and glass-blowing:** workshops in the village of Sant Rafel.
** **Cliff walks:** around Cala Bassa.
* **The Cave Aquarium:** unusual cave setting.

Opposite: *Sant Antoni mostly attracts visitors in search of sun, fun and limitless nightlife.*

Best buys

Fashion: Straw bags from Ibiza's markets. Ad Lib fashion is available in the boutiques all around Eivissa.
Jewellery: Gold and silver jewellery, particularly earrings and bracelets, is available from the craft markets and often imitates the traditional Ibizenco style derived from Moorish designs that are 1000 years old.
Ceramics: Sold along the roadsides, locally made pottery is bright and colourful. It is also very bulky to pack! Other good buys include *hierbas*, the local digestif; locally made herbs and spices and otherwise expensive herbs and spices like saffron (*azafran*).

Sant Antoni

Sant Antoni Town **

Sant Antoni's huge bay is one of the busiest ports in the Balearics. The vast natural harbour was named **Portus Magnus** by the Romans and a derivative of that name is used today in the resort's full name, **Sant Antoni de Portmany**. The resort is also known as **Sant Antoni Abad**.

In the early 1960s, before Ibiza was discovered by hippies and travellers, Sant Antoni was a tiny fishing village nestled around a 14th-century church at the northern end of the bay. As early visitors discovered its exquisite beaches and fiery sunsets, the resort began to expand, eventually stretching right round the bay. The development is in 1960s fashion, with concrete skyscrapers rather than the pretty whitewashed villas that are characteristic of the island.

Although the style is more neon than natural, Sant Antoni fills a much-needed niche. The low prices, frantic nightlife and buzzing atmosphere make the resort popular with teenagers and young people on their first parent-free holiday.

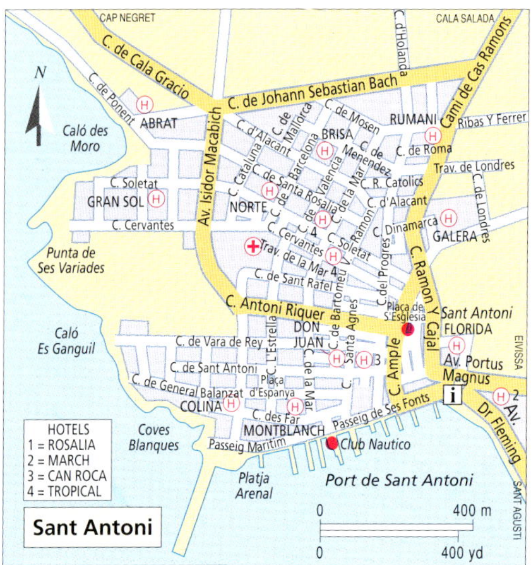

The Harbour **

The harbour here is a constant source of fascination. Inter-island ferries, taxi boats taking visitors to the bays around the coast, and the occasional container ship come and go throughout the day.

The **Passeig Maritim** is a long seafront promenade lined with cafés and bars, their outdoor seating shaded by palm trees. Inline skaters buzz up and down, and in the evening this is a popular spot for a more leisurely *passeig*.

Old Town **

The older part of town is now swallowed up by the shops and hotels a few blocks back from the promenade. It centres on a collection of pretty stucco houses clustered around a solid-looking white church, dating back to the 14th century and, with its fortified tower, resembling a tiny fortress. Like many Ibizenco churches, the structure is simple with clean lines and a minimalist interior. The church's peaceful setting amidst colourful gardens seems far removed from the bustling resort that has enveloped it.

A few more old buildings, stately crumbling mansions, still stand towards the northern end of the promenade. Look out for **Villa Mercedes** near the Club Nautico, a lovely old house in a tangle of overgrown gardens with blue and white tiles adorning its faded walls.

Above: *The port of Sant Antoni is among the busiest in the Balearics.*
Below: *The Church, a haven of quiet, dates to the 14th century.*

Sant Antoni itself does not have much beach to speak of and much of its charm lies in exploring the little bays around the coast by boat. There are, however, a few beaches around **Cala de Bou**, the long, horseshoe-shaped bay. Next to the Passeig Maritim is the **Platja Arenal**, a stretch of soft sand that gets very, very busy, and beyond that lie four or five other spots of gently shelving sand. A road runs the entire length of the bay with free parking on one side, so there's no danger of being towed.

Above: *San An nightlife winds up slowly, beginning early in the evening with a visit to a bar.*

Seafood Terminology

Fabulous seafood is available all around Sant Antoni but certain Catalan / Eivissenc words may be unfamiliar.
Bacallà: dried cod
Lluc: hake
Cloises: clams
Tonyina: tuna
Truita: trout, often stuffed with ham
Pop: octopus
Rap: monkfish
Llagosta: lobster
Guisat de peix: fish and shellfish stew.

San An Nights

Sant Antoni comes alive as the sun leaves a scarlet glow in the sky and the last boats chug back into the harbour to disgorge their cargo of sunworshippers. Finding somewhere authentically Ibizenco to eat is not very easy, with most holidaymakers being content to settle for pizza and chips, but Sant Antoni does have some excellent restaurants amidst the glitter of all the neon.

For early evening drinks, nothing beats the **Café del Mar**, Ibiza's original sunset-watching venue. **Mambo** on Vara del Rey, **Mezzanine Sunset Bar** and **Club Nautic** on the Passeig Maritimo are also popular pre-dinner chill-out venues. At Port d'es Torrent, try **Kumharas**, where there are hammocks, hippies, a variety of Asian food and sculptures.

For dinner, some of the best restaurants are out of town. **Can Pujol**, located as far as you can go around the bay from the West End, is little more than a beach shack but serves giant seafood platters and has great sunset views. **El Chiringuito** on Cala Gracioneta serves Mediteranean specialities under the pine trees by candlelight, while Cala Salada, located on a beautiful beach, cooks its fish over a wood fire.

Further outside the town, **C'an Berri** serves local specialities in a lovely old Spanish house with tables outside. Then, of course, there's **Pikes**, a luxury hotel with an excellent restaurant. Frequented by rock stars and other celebrities, the hotel lies nestled in the hills outside Sant Antoni. **Sa Capella** is an atmospheric establishment in an old church, while **Sa Tasca**, heading out of town on the Sant Josep road, has stunning views from its terrace.

Nightclubs ★★★

By midnight, San An's West End is positively teeming with people as public relations teams from all the discos try to tempt visitors with offers ranging from cheap cocktails to two drinks for the price of one. **Eden** and **Es Paradis** are the two big clubs, located close to each other on Carrer Salvador Esperiu. Es Paradis is especially spectacular, with marble staircases, a sunken dance floor and giant palms giving it the air of a Grecian temple.

Family Entertainment

Children tend to go to bed much later in Spain than anywhere else, and you'll often see families out and about as late as midnight. The big clubs are entirely unsuitable but nevertheless there are plenty of bars in the area that welcome children. **Maxims** is a family-orientated bar which offers table football and pool; the **Bull Bar** on the bay has a rodeo ride and a nightclub. The **Rodeo Fun Park** is very good for families as it has laser karaoke, sports satellite TV, and also a number of trampolines for children. A bowling club is open until late at the **Buccanero Kid**, a log cabin with its effect slightly marred by the ubiquitous flashing neon signs. In the afternoons, take the Ibitren miniature railway from the Columbus egg to Santa Ires and El Mirador, for great views.

The Sant Antoni Egg

On the main roundabout of Sant Antoni, a miniature model of a ship sits inside a giant concrete egg. The story behind the egg is thus: Columbus, who was believed to be from Ibiza (as well as Mallorca and various parts of the Spanish mainland!), was seeking finance for an expedition to Asia. On being told it was an impossible task, he retorted with an offer to make an egg stand upright, another impossible task. Columbus then cracked the base of the egg and stood it on one end. The would-be backers were so impressed with his approach to problem solving that they came up with the money.

Above: *Columbus' achievements are playfully celebrated by the Sant Antoni egg.*
Left: *Go-karting, near Sant Antoni, keeps kids amused for hours.*

How to Fit in in Ibiza

Want to join the beautiful people? Here are some basics:
- Dress outrageously in the evenings, preferably in white
- Charter a yacht for the day
- Never eat before 22:00 or turn up at a club before 01:00
- Take your *passeig* in Eivissa at sunset, stopping in the 'Ibiza Triangle' for a cocktail
- Stay in the Dalt Vila, or rent an apartment there for the summer
- Have lunch at Malibu in Ses Salines
- See an Ad Lib fashion show
- Be seen in Pikes, having a drink
- Visit Pacha in the evening (where you will have to make one glass of champagne last all night unless you really are rich).

Beaches North of Sant Antoni

Boats leave throughout the day from the Passeig Maritim to the *calas* around Sant Antoni, either according to a schedule or simply when they are full. Most have a shade on deck, but put on plenty of sunscreen as the rays bouncing off the water can be dazzling.

Cala Gració ★★

Just 2km (1¼ miles) north of Sant Antoni off the Santa Inés road, a turning to the left leads to the two pretty coves of Cala Gració and its tiny neighbour, Cala Grassioneta. The beaches extend back to some shady pine trees and there are roped-off swimming areas to protect children from the windsurfers attracted to this sheltered spot. A handful of *chiringuitas* (beach bars) supply sustenance to the sunbathers and there are rocks to explore at the end of the beach. Take out a pedalo and look back at the contrast of turquoise water, ochre sand and bottle-green pines – a truly breathtaking vista.

Camping

Ibiza has seven campsites. There are two at Sant Antoni (one of which is at the pretty Cala Bassa); one at Platja d'en Bossa; three in the pine woods around Santa Eulària and two at Cala Portinatx in the far north. All the campsites have facilities and shade. Camping is prohibited on Formentera. Some people camp in fields and on beaches but the fields invariably belong to someone and the beaches may be patrolled by police, who will move the offenders on. Staying in a designated campsite is cheap, anyway, and puts less pressure on the environment.

Around Cala Salada ***

One of the island's most captivating coves, Cala Salada lies 4km (2½ miles) to the north of Sant Antoni. Its crystal-clear water reflects the blue sky as an astonishing shade of turquoise while the beach itself is tiny, formed of soft sand with rocks at either side leading to further hidden bays. The sandy sea floor slopes away gently, making this beach safe for children, and there is some colourful underwater life around the rocks.

Cala Salada can be reached either by boat or by road; the road is asphalt all the way and the cycle ride fairly gentle. You can even walk: a coastal path of sorts leads from Cala Gració, itself only a short bus ride from Sant Antoni, to Cala Salada and takes about one and a half hours across high cliffs and hidden coves with plenty of picnic spots en route.

If travelling by car, make time for some diversions off the main road. The drive is spectacular with flashes of aquamarine sea through the pine trees, and in spring an endless sea of pinky-white almond blossom snows on the rust-coloured earth. In the village of Santa Agnès there's a Paleochristian church, now a national monument, and next to it a second church has been converted into a restaurant. Take time to follow the dirt tracks to the left off this road; the coast side of the thick pine woods frequently reveals wonderful unexpected scenery.

Further north, about 10km (6 miles) outside Sant Antoni, on top of the wild Cap Nonó, there's a signpost for **Ses Fontanelles**, a cave with Bronze Age paintings on the walls. It is always open to visitors,

Opposite: *A rough coastal path leads north from picturesque Cala Gració.*
Left: *While exploring the coast, it's worth taking diversions. This windmill is situated just outside Sant Antoni.*

Safe Tanning

The Mediterranean sun is very strong. Always wear a high-protection sunscreen – medical guidelines now recommend at least factor 15 with UVA and UVB screens – and keep out of the sun between 11:00 and 15:00. Remember that once you have spent the time in the sun permitted by the sunscreen, i.e. 40 minutes with factor two or three, or a couple of hours with factor 15, further applications will not protect your skin from burning. Children should always wear a sunhat and a close-weave T-shirt. Be even more careful when on a boat as the sun's rays reflect off the water. Drink plenty of water during the day to avoid dehydration and use a good moisturizer in the evening to soothe any sunburn.

Above: *Dark-yellow sand at Cala Bassa, a highly popular beach in summer.*
Opposite: *Several beaches on Ibiza have been awarded Blue Flags.*

> **SQUID**
>
> Squid, or *calamares*, is eaten everywhere on Ibiza and Formentera. Keen snorkellers may catch a few in a net and if you want to cook it yourself, the most typical way is to stew it in its own ink. Alternatively, dry the squid in the sun for 12 hours and grill it on the barbecue with a squeeze of lemon juice. Most people are pretty squeamish, however, when it comes to hunting and gathering, and enjoy it more if prepared by somebody else.

South of Sant Antoni

There are four beautiful bays situated to the west of Sant Antoni around a sandstone headland at the end of **Cala de Bou**. All of them are accessible by road, albeit dirt track in some cases, and by boat from Sant Antoni.

Cala Bassa **

Take the **Port des Torrent** road from Sant Antoni and follow the signs to Cala Bassa. The route may seem haphazard but the cove is well signposted and once out of town, the road passes through unspoiled countryside of fruit orchards, red-ploughed fields, white cube-like houses and, hidden in the pine-clad hills, some smart-looking villas. On the right-hand side of the country lane heading down to Cala Bassa there's a yoga centre, offering total escape in a peaceful setting. A week at the centre includes two classes a day and freshly made vegetarian food.

Cala Bassa itself is a fairly mainstream beach that gets busy in summer. A wide stretch of dark-yellow sand at the sheltered end of a deep cove, the beach offers shade under some trees and is flanked to the right by a series of flat, rocky platforms, perfect for sand-free sunbathing. There are plenty of facilities here, from sunbeds to watersports and beach volleyball, but the sand remains clean and unspoiled.

Beyond Cala Bassa, dirt tracks weave all over the scrub-covered hills, and a couple of ramshackle bars make a wonderful spot to watch the sunset as the last boats chug back to Sant Antoni and the lights begin to come on around the bay. The wind- and sand-blasted cliffs are a dramatic shade of ochre and the water so clear that, from the clifftop, you can count the black sea urchins on the sea bed.

Blue Flag Beaches

Ibiza has several Blue Flag beaches, an accolade awarded by the European Community (EC) for a beach of exceptional standard. Cala Sant Miquel in the northwest is one such beach. The criteria for qualification are: unpolluted and regularly analyzed water; cleaning of sand and litter bins; access for the disabled; drinking water; lifeguard on duty; beach showers; first aid point; the banning of animals, camping and vehicles on the sand; and a tourist information point. A flag with a distinctive blue logo flies to indicate that the beach has qualified.

Illa Conillera *

Conillera is a rocky slab of an island in the bay of Sant Antoni. Now uninhabited, the island is, according to local legend, the birthplace of **Hannibal**, the Carthaginian general (though like Columbus, Hannibal has numerous alleged birthplaces). The lighthouse on Conillera comes on automatically at dusk and can be seen from miles away. From the clifftops outside Sant Antoni, you can usually spot a couple of yachts moored at a tiny inlet there. Good for picnics, the island provides a real escape from the crowds as lizards and birds are its only inhabitants. A carpet of wild flowers in spring adds to the island's beauty and on warmer days, the rocky sea floor makes for good snorkelling.

Platjes de Conta **

More beautiful Caribbean-like beaches line the coast around the rocky headland that faces Illa Conillera. The **Platjes de Conta** form a stretch of fine sand, almost 800m (½ mile) long, interspersed with

> **GESTURES**
>
> Some gestures in a Spaniard's wide repertoire are self-explanatory: pursing the fingertips and kissing them, for example, means 'this is wonderful'. Others have obscure origins. The way to say 'Let's have a drink' is to make a fist with the thumb and little finger extended, imitating the action of drinking from a *bota*, or leather drinking bottle. A hand with the first and fourth finger raised, meanwhile, means someone has been unfaithful, the fingers representing the horns of the devil which tempted the cuckold.

rocks. The gently sloping seabed has the occasional deep spot for snorkelling. This area never gets very crowded outside of high season and to escape from the sunbathers that do discover it, simply walk along the cliff path towards Cala Bassa. When the path disappears on the stony ground, head towards the **Torre d'en Rovira**, an ancient watchtower that is in a remarkably good state of preservation. The scenery is indescribably beautiful up here, especially in spring when gorse bushes add splashes of yellow and wild thyme and rosemary scent the air. Be careful not to walk too close to the cliff edge: centuries of being gently eroded by the sea means that you may be balancing on an overhang and the odd rock slide is not unheard of.

Cala Codolar *

Another charming little cove, Cala Codolar is slightly busier in summer than Conta because of its proximity to a holiday village. There are quite a few facilities on the boulder-strewn beach and dinghies and windsurfers are available for hire.

Left: *Foam lets rip inside Amnesia, one of the most famous nightclubs in the world.*

Opposite: *Glassware for sale in Sant Rafel village, inland from Sant Antoni.*

Sant Rafel de sa Geu**

A few kilometres inland from Sant Antoni, the sleepy hamlet of **Sant Rafel** probably never reckoned on becoming a major pilgrimage for clubbers from all over Europe. By day, Sant Rafel is little more than a string of whitewashed houses and a peaceful little church basking in the sun. A few tourist attractions have sprung up: Sant Rafel is famous for its potteries and there are several ceramicas where you can buy attractive pots and urns at good prices.

At night everything changes. Disco buses bring truckloads of revellers to the island's two most famous attractions, **Privilege** (formerly KU) and **Amnesia**, giant barn-like nightclubs outside the village.

Privilege has to be seen to be believed. Owned by Brazilians, it looks like a vast railway station and holds a staggering 9000 people. The club has everything: restaurants, shops, numerous bars, a swimming pool and acres of dance floor – all on a spectacular scale. Space-age rigging flies high above the dancers illuminated by dazzling light shows, a DJ travels up and down in a glass lift, and techno music thuds out at trance-making volume. Across the road, **Amnesia** is like a giant greenhouse built around an old *finca* and featuring a lush tropical garden. Spectacular theme parties are held regularly at Amnesia and some mornings at around 03:00 there's the famous **foam party** where foam pours thick over the dance floor, showering thousands of sweaty bodies.

Safe Clubbing

Drugs of any kind are illegal in Spain and the penalties for possession are severe. Inevitably, though, hard drugs are evident in Ibiza's club scene. If you must take Ecstasy, be aware that it can kill and that you don't know what you're buying or taking. Do not take an E on top of excessive alcohol. Always in any case drink plenty of water in the clubs to avoid dehydration, particularly after a day on the beach. Also watch out for your friends at foam parties. These have been banned in London and other European capitals as people have been crushed in the crowd and hidden by the foam.

Sant Antoni at a Glance

Best Times To Visit

Sant Antoni is very much a summer resort and from October to May many of the attractions, hotels and restaurants are closed as well as the big clubs.

If you're not after nightlife, **May** is a wonderful month when the countryside is at its most beautiful and the beach restaurants quiet. July and August are hot and packed.

Local saints' days:
Sant Antoni, 17 January,
Sant Bartomeu, 24 August.

Getting There

From the airport, the best option is a **taxi**. The journey takes about 25 minutes. **Car rental** is also available at the airport and the route to Sant Antoni crosses the island via the main road. Alternatively, take a **bus** to Eivissa and connect to a Sant Antoni bus there.

Getting Around

Sant Antoni is served by the excellent local **bus service**, website: www.ibizabus.com
The **Discobus** leaves on the hour for Eivissa and Sant Rafel from 00:00–06:00, tel: 971 19 24 56.

Voramar El Gaucho, tel: 971 34 03 82, has local services to the *calas* around the coast. Alternatively, hire a **bicycle**, **car** or **motorbike** in the resort.

Ferries sail from Sant Antoni to mainland Spain and Mallorca. There are plenty of local boat services to the beaches and bays around the coast from the marina opposite the taxi rank.

Where to Stay

As Sant Antoni is the centre of Ibiza's package tour industry, most hotels block-book rooms in advance to tour operators throughout the summer. Finding anything other than luxury accommodation independently, particularly on spec, is very difficult. Booking in advance or through a tour operator is strongly advised.

Luxury

Pikes,
Camí de Sa Vorera, Sant Antoni, tel: 971 34 22 22, fax: 971 34 23 12. Luxurious, rambling country house on hill overlooking Sant Antoni. Popular with showbiz personalities. Excellent restaurant.

Hotel Nautilus,
Badia de Sant Antoni, tel: 971 34 04 00, fax: 971 34 04 02. Smart hotel on the bay.

Mid-range

Yoga Centre,
Cala Bassa, tel: 971 34 29 67. Yoga retreats and holidays in a beautiful setting.

Hotel Victoria,
Apartado de Correos 295, Sant Josep, tel: 971 34 09 00. Charming 'aparthotel' high above Sant Antoni bay.

Club-Hotel Tarida Beach,
Platja de Cala Tarida, tel: 971 80 03 40. Three-star property on the beautiful Tarida Beach outside Sant Antoni.

Hotel Cap Nono,
Crtra Port des Torrent, tel: 971 34 07 50. Three-star hotel on the remote Cap Nonó, north of Sant Antoni. Car hire recommended.

La Torre,
Cap Negret, tel: 971 34 22 71. Bed and breakfast with hammocks, 20 minutes walk from town.

Hotel Es Pla,
Avda Portus Magnus, tel: 971 34 11 54, fax: 971 34 04 52. Large, modern hotel, three minutes' walk from town centre.

Hotel Marco Polo,
Avda Portus Magnus, tel: 971 34 10 50. Sister hotel to the Es Pla.

Hotel Cala Gració,
Platja de Cala Gració, tel/fax: 971 34 08 62. Three-star hotel on picturesque beach outside Sant Antoni.

Budget

Mitjorn,
c/des far 6, tel: 971 34 09 02. Basic *hostal* set back from the harbour.

Hotel Prima,
Carrer Soledad 56, tel: 971 34 06 26. Basic but friendly *hostal* within walking distance of town centre.

Sant Antoni at a Glance

Where to Eat

Sa Tasca, San Augustín, Sant Josép, tel: 971 34 37 03. Nouvelle cuisine and lots of flambéed dishes in rustic but elegant setting.

La Luna de Miel, Sant Rafel, tel: 971 31 19 23.

Sa Capella, Puig den Barosa, Crtra a Cala Salada, tel: 971 34 00 57. Local specialities in an old church. Charming but expensive.

Can Pujol, Badia de Sant Antoni, tel: 971 34 14 07. Rustic fish restaurant on quiet beach with superb local specialities.

Paris, Carrer del Progrés, Sant Antoni, tel: 971 34 00 18. Island specialities in old part of Sant Antoni. Popular with locals.

Rincon del Pepe, Carrer Sant Mateo, Sant Antoni, tel: 971 34 06 97. Tapas bar one block back from seafront. Spanish cuisine served on vine-covered terrace.

Restaurant Cala Salada, Cala Salada, tel: 971 34 28 67. Good beach restaurant to the north of Sant Antoni. Fish and snacks cooked in wood-fired oven.

Cas Mila, Cala Tarida, tel: 971 80 61 93. Sophisticated seafood restaurant on the beach. Open evenings and lunchtime.

Sa Soca, Crtra San Josep km2, tel: 971 34 16 20. Country restaurant outside Sant Antoni serving local game specialities.

Grill Magnon, Port des Torrent, tel: 971 34 02 98. Island specialities, including roast suckling pig and grills, served on large garden terrace.

Nightlife

Privilege, Crtra Eivissa–Sant Antoni km7, tel: 971 19 22 33. Ibiza's most famous night-club. Open from May–October. Expensive.

Amnesia, As above, km6 (opposite Privilege on Eivissa–Sant Antoni road); website: www.amnesia.es

Es Paradis, Avinguda Dr Fleming, Sant Antoni, tel: 971 34 66 00, website: www.esparadis.com Big, popular club under glass pyramid on Sant Antoni bay.

Café del Mar, Essential gathering place in Sant Antoni before clubbing.

Shopping

Shops in **Sant Antoni** are predictably touristy but you can still find a good selection of 'quality' souvenirs, such as Majorica fake pearls from Mallorca and Lladro porcelain.

Sant Rafel is good for ceramics, sold at the many roadside *ceramicas*, and glassware from the **Castell des Puig** glass-blowing centre. **Privilege** has a boutique selling clubbing T-shirts and memorabilia.

Tours and Excursions

Tour companies run trips to Eivissa with guided tours of Dalt Vila, as well as island tours that visit some of the *calas*. **Boats** leave regularly for the more remote *calas*. If you sail, charter a yacht and sail to **Illa Conillera** for lunch away from the crowds. Children will enjoy the **Cave Aquarium** at the very top end of the Passeig Maritim, an aquarium in a deep natural cave (as its name suggests).

Useful Contacts

Tourist office, Passeig de ses Fonts s/n, tel: 971 34 33 63, fax: 971 34 41 76.

Sailing school: Club Nautico de Sant Antoni, Passeig Maritim s/n, tel: 971 34 06 45.

Diving: Underwater Activity Club of Ibiza and Formentera, tel: 971 33 15 15. Organized dives and tuition. There is a decom-pression chamber in Sant Antoni at Club La Sirena, tel: 971 34 07 18.

Horse racing: Trotting races at the **Sant Rafel Hippo-drome**, tel: 971 19 81 93.

Captain Nemo boat-trips, tel: 971 34 44 49.

San Antonio go-karts, tel: 971 34 38 05.

4
Santa Eulària and Surrounds

Ibiza's third-largest town with a population of 16,000, **Santa Eulària** is more of a community than Sant Antoni. Its population is more established and permanent. Located on the island's east coast, the town boasts the only flowing river in the Balearics, from which it takes its full name of Santa Eulària del Riú. Although the river is dry in summer, it plays an important role in irrigating the surrounding farmland for the rest of the year and provides a tranquil setting for a picnic.

The original hippies who arrived in the 1960s were drawn to the area by the beauty of the rolling countryside, the pretty white *fincas* and the tranquil coves. They settled in the village of **Sant Carles** to the north of Santa Eulària. Some of these same hippies still man the craft stalls at the weekly hippie market in **Punta Arabi** just outside the town. It was also in this area that **Es Canar** was developed by a British family as one of the island's first holiday resorts.

Like most of the coastline, the scenery around Santa Eulària consists of sandy beaches, deep fjords, steep cliffs and pine-clad headlands. Inland, however, the countryside is softer and more undulating than further north or south. Dirt tracks crisscross orange and lemon groves, orchards of olive trees and fields of crops. Life in Santa Eulària moves at a leisurely pace, attracting families and older visitors who are drawn to the town's rustic ambience and many excellent restaurants. Buses connect Santa Eulària to Sant Antoni and Eivissa and the wild scenery of the north is within easy driving distance.

Don't Miss

*** **The hippie market:** held weekly at Punta Arabi.
*** **Santa Eulària's restaurants:** many excellent options.
** **Sant Carles:** a pretty, sleepy village once frequented by artists and hippies.
** **Santa Eulària's parish church:** perched high on Puig de Missa.
* **Cala Mastella:** one of the most beautiful, unspoilt beaches.

Opposite: *Outside town, Puig de Missa is the site of Santa Eulària's sturdy parish church.*

PARISH CHURCHES

Two centuries ago, the parish church was the focal point of each village and was designed as such. (It is for this reason that virtually every village has a religious name.) As farms were so scattered, an attempt was made to draw people into communities and at the same time, afford some protection against the many pirate raids. The churches themselves are modest in design but sturdy, resembling mini-fortresses, and always have a shaded porch, designed as a gathering place for locals to catch up on gossip.

SANTA EULÀRIA

Santa Eulària is a sprawling town with several areas of interest to visitors. A tiny *rambla,* modelled on its namesake in Barcelona, stretches from the Ajuntament (Town Hall) to the seafront. The new marina attracts a yachting crowd, and the streets parallel to the sea a few blocks inland are packed with restaurants and shops.

Puig de Missa **

Santa Eulària's focal point, although outside the town, is its parish church, built high on a hill in order to keep a lookout for approaching pirate ships. The church was built in 1568 on the site of an old chapel that had been destroyed by Turkish pirates, and was designed by Calvi, the architect responsible for the walls around Dalt Vila in Eivissa. Puig de Missa, meanwhile, takes its name from the flour mills that used to be characteristic of the area – the remains of which can still be seen today. The solid-looking church has a fortified tower, to ensure that it would not meet the same fate as its predecessor and could provide shelter for the local peasants in the event of a pirate raid. Typical Ibizenco, cube-shaped houses, their gardens bright with scarlet geraniums and purple bougainvillea, are clustered around the church. This ensemble has captured the imagination of countless artists and photographers, many of whom settled here, and the little cemetery contains many French, German and English names, among them the American writer Elliot Paul, whose book, *Life and Death in a Spanish Town,* describes life in Santa Eulària in the 1930s.

Ethnological museum *

There's a tiny museum on Puig de Missa in **C'an Ros** which contains costumes, jewellery, tools, weapons and musical instruments. It is a fascinating showcase of the town's history, and well worth a visit. Open 11:00–13:00 and 17:00–19:00, closed Sunday and Monday morning.

Above: *An ethnological museum faithfully documents the history of Santa Eulària.*

Puig Musona **

From the church, you can climb on up the **Puig Musona**, the wooded hill behind the town. Follow the signs to **Ermita Puig de sa Creu**. A path zigzags up the hill through the pine woods to a tiny white chapel, once an Islamic shrine. The views from here up and down the coast are magnificent.

Roman Bridge *

Outside the town, two bridges cross the river. The older one was constructed by the **Romans** in AD70. The area was inhabited even earlier than this by **Carthaginians** who exploited lead mines around Sant Carles. The mines were only closed at the beginning of the 19th century but the tunnels that remain are unstable and dangerous.

Walking Around Town

Exploring Santa Eulària on foot is very simple. One main street, **Carrer Sant Jaume**, runs parallel to the sea and perpendicular to the tiny *rambla*. Shops and cafés are located here. Behind the main road, however, is a culinary adventure on the pedestrianized **Sant Vicent**, a lane of pretty, whitewashed houses containing one excellent restaurant after another. On a summer night, the street is packed with people strolling along, studying restaurant menus or gossiping over wine and tapas.

Island Fruits

A number of delicious fruits are in season during the summer. Try huge bunches of grapes for a picnic lunch, or giant slices of thirst-quenching watermelon. Peaches and nectarines are big and juicy in the summer and, in May, every restaurant has *fresas con nata*, strawberries with cream, on the menu.
February and March are good months for freshly squeezed orange juice from Ibiza's orchards and, in October, you can eat the yellow fruit from the prickly pear cactus. If you are thinking about picking prickly pear yourself, be careful, as it is poisonous if not ripe, and is covered in hundreds of tiny, insidious spikes. Also look out for fresh pomegranates and figs, both grown locally.

Above: *The older of Santa Eulària's two bridges was built in Roman times.*
Opposite: *A perennially popular destination, Es Canar is great for families.*

Eating and Drinking

Try the **Bar Los Amigos** for delicious tapas. Very atmospheric, it's always busy with local people and the waiters don't speak English – not a problem as you point to the tapas displayed on the bar. Garlic and strings of chillies hang from the ceiling and every inch of wall is covered with postcards and fading photographs of Spanish celebrities.

Ca Na Ribes also serves local specialities while, for a change, **Maharba** serves Arabic-style *meze* to guests lounging on cushions at long, low tables.

The biggest treat, however, is an evening sampling the incredible array of tapas at **Rincon de Pepe**, a cozy, dark, traditional bar/restaurant run by the eponymous and very jolly Pepe. The menu changes daily but things to look out for include *boquerones* – anchovies fried in a light batter – grilled asparagus and wild mushrooms with garlic.

More bars and restaurants are located down by the marina, a modern development that attracts a lot of attention in summer. There are several good restaurants here and some very lively bars, including the **Alhambra Café**, an Arabic-themed bar with lots of cushions and good Turkish coffee.

THE DEVIL'S BRIDGE

Although Santa Eulària's bridge was built by the Romans, a local legend suggests that the Devil himself built it in one night, in return for the soul of the first person to walk across it. Strangely, the same legend exists around a similar Roman bridge on the mainland, in Catalunya. Devil or no devil, there are some pretty picnic spots under the Santa Eulària bridge along the banks of the river, where wild fennel and thyme perfume the air.

Beaches *

There are two beaches in Santa Eulària: the main town beach in front of the *rambla*, and the rather unusual beach immediately south of this one where the river meets the sea. Sun loungers are lined up along a spit of white sand created by the river depositing silt and pebbles (when it flows), and there are some interesting spots along the banks for one to explore or have a quiet picnic at, overhung by shady trees.

Es Canar *

Essentially a family resort, Es Canar is quieter and more sedate than other parts of the coast. Built around a wide, sandy bay thick with pines, the resort was started in 1964 by the Hayes family, originally from Britain, who built the Hotel Panorama. The road to Santa Eulària used to be a dirt track; sheep grazed outside the hotel; and there was no electricity, telephone or water. Eivissa was a four-hour trek away. Visitors nonetheless fell in love with the place and Es Canar slowly built up to its present state: a busy, very English resort where every other restaurant serves bacon and eggs or Yorkshire pudding. Nightlife is less frenetic than in Sant Antoni, although there are a couple of clubs, and most people spend the evenings in the hotels or walking the wide sweep of the promenade, past the sandy beach and tiny marina where old wooden fishing boats bob in the clear water.

Taxis

Taxis on Ibiza have meters but a printed tariff is often used instead, usually posted at the taxi rank. An illuminated green light on the taxi means it is free. Taxis wait at ranks in all the main towns but can also be hailed on the street. If you take the bus to a remote beach, however, make a note of the last return time as taxis do not stray off the main roads. A tip of around 10% is appropriate for friendly service but not expected. Some drivers take advantage of tourists who are not familiar with Spanish money and 'mistakenly' short-change them. If you have cause to complain, take the cab registration number and report the driver to the tourist office.

Superstitions

Some of Ibiza's superstitions are so peculiar that their roots have never been traced. For example, if a (fictitious) seed sprouted and then died in a green bottle on the morning of St. John's day, according to legend, it would turn into an elf. Elves had to be supplied with plentiful food and work to keep them out of mischief and were useful for doing odd jobs around the house. Another odd belief is that the news of the death of a relative must be spread to one person at a time. If no one is available to pass the news on to, an object like a tree or a rock must be told to prevent the death of the messenger in the following year.

Many of the hotels here have children's clubs which entertain kids for the day with treasure hunts, games and face painting. For adults, small boat taxis make regular trips around the headland to Cala Llonga and there are regular buses into Santa Eulària with good connections on to Eivissa. To explore the more remote north, a car or bicycle is needed but there are some pleasant walking trails around the rocky headlands.

Walk to Cala Llenya **

This walk to a pretty cove to the north of Es Canar is ideal for early evening or a cooler day outside the main summer season. The walk takes about an hour although you may want to stop to sunbathe or swim on the way.

Walk along the beach promenade towards the north and around the headland, which is in the process of being developed. A coastal footpath continues outside the new hotels there and you'll often see people fishing off the rocks. The bay next to Es Canar is distinguished by a column-like rock offshore. After about 20 minutes you should have passed this bay.

Opposite: *Wonderfully clear water around Es Canar satisfies swimmers and sunbathers alike.*
Left: *The hippie market at Es Canar began as a fund-raising exercise for a local school.*

Continue along the coastal footpath to **Punta Verde**, another small beach backed by pine woods. The bay is blissfully quiet. Once past the Las Perlas apartments, the trail becomes an asphalt road. Turn right, follow the line of the Las Perlas swimming pool and head back towards the sea. The coastal scenery now becomes more rugged as the path follows rocky cliffs. A small stony cove comes into view and after a slight uphill trail through the pine woods, so does the sandy beach of **Cala Llenya**. At the opposite end of the bay, a flight of steps leads up to Club Platja Azul, a holiday village set amidst beautiful, subtropical gardens. Buses from here go back to Es Canar.

Hippie Market ★★★

The hippie market in Es Canar is a weekly attraction for visitors. **Punta Arabi**, where it takes place, is a shady, pine-clad headland just outside Es Canar over which a pretty bungalow development sprawls under the shade of the trees. Popular with Germans, the village specializes in young people's holidays but every Wednesday, it is

MAY DAY CELEBRATIONS

Santa Eulària's flower festival, held on the first weekend of May, was once an island-wide event heralding the arrival of spring and probably based on an ancient fertility rite. Now confined to just one parish, the festival runs over a weekend, the most important event being a parade of carriages through the town centre, each one festooned with flowers. Visitors will see people walking or driving through the town bearing spectacular pot plants and flower arrangements; each year, a show and competition are held in one of the town's hotels. In the evening, local bands and rock groups play on a temporary stage outside the Ajuntament (town hall) and the tiny *rambla* throngs with life.

transformed into a replica of the 1960s as Ibiza's few remaining, rather ancient hippies sell their wares alongside more commercially minded entrepreneurs. Coaches come from all over the island and special boats run from Eivissa and Sant Antoni on market day.

The market began in the late 1960s as a fund-raising exercise for a local school. The timing was good, as the normally placid islanders had begun to complain about the languorous, 'stoned' lifestyle of Ibiza's hippies. The market served as an outlet for local arts, crafts and household items, and the island's developing style. It also provided a focus for those hippies who travelled the 'hippie trail' to India in winter and came back laden with goods to sell.

What is on display today is somewhat removed from the market's origins, but is nonetheless tremendous fun. Endless stalls of silver jewellery line the pathways, as well as clothing with vivid tie-dye patterns, rarely seen outside Ibiza, Goa or California. There's pottery, paintings, woven bracelets, embroidered waistcoats, candlesticks, glassware, belts, bags and leather clothing. If you want something authentic, ask where it was made; pottery, for example, is often imported from the mainland as there is no clay on Ibiza.

Modern souvenirs can be just as much fun. One stall sells big posters from the nightclubs and 'Ibiza dance mixes' on compact disc. There are sand pictures, hair beading and braiding, freshly squeezed orange juice, burgers, the ubiquitous fake Rolexes as well as some good, cheap modern jewellery. As for hippies, there are still a few stallholders with the requisite beaded hair and faraway expression, although only a small community of hippies resides on the island today. The occasional entrepreneurs can be spotted in all the gear, strumming The Mamas and the Papas songs on guitars and ostentatiously smoking huge joints.

Hippie Life

Middle-aged hippies today remember the days when they would spend happy, hazy summers in white *fincas* around Sant Carles and travel to Goa, India, for the winters to amass trinkets which they would sell in the hippie market. Everybody hung out in Anita's Bar or, on Sunday mornings, would gather at Sandy's in Eivissa. Those who worked were painters, fashion designers and 'resting' actors. Amnesia was a sleepy *finca* with a barbecue; Privilege was a bar with a sound system and a pool. Platja d'en Bossa was just an empty beach.

SANT CARLES **

The village of **Sant Carles de Peralta** is set in some of Ibiza's most beautiful countryside with rolling fields brilliant with poppies in spring, rich orchards, pine woods and idyllic white farmhouses dotted around the country lanes. Charcoal burning used to be the main industry here and on a walk across the fields, you'll often stumble across a ring of stones set around an earthern mound, all that remains of a very labour-intensive industry.

It was in Sant Carles that the hippies chose to settle in the 1960s, often living 20 to one *finca* and farming cannabis, which was met with puzzlement by the islanders. **Bar Anita**, a onetime hippie hangout, is still going strong, serving Ibizenco specialities and *hierbas*, the local liqueur. **Las Dalias**, another hippie special, has live music at weekends and a more authentic craft market than the main market.

Sant Carles itself is little but a couple of streets lined with whitewashed houses. At the centre there's a tiny, immaculately kept church which was built in the 18th century. Its cool interior beckons in the heat of the day. Three crosses on the front resemble the Passion and there's an equally small bell tower.

Cala Mastella **

Cala Mastella is typical of Ibizenco coastal scenery: a beautiful, tranquil fjord with wooded headlands to either side and a tiny sandy beach.

BEST BEACHES FOR ESCAPISTS

Want to get away from the crowds? Try the following:
Cala Mastella: exquisite beach near Sant Carles with two excellent restaurants, one hidden behind the rocks to the left.
Platja de Comte: beautiful and deserted with basic facilities. Shallow water with some rocks for snorkelling and flat rocks on either side of the beach for sunbathing.
Cala de Benirras: incredibly beautiful beach at the base of steep cliffs near Sant Miquel. Good walking.
Cala des Cubells: narrow, boulder-strewn beach down a bumpy track.

Opposite: *By no means all the stalls at the hippie market have lost their authenticity.*
Left: *Sant Carles village is tiny but has an immaculate 18th-century church.*

Mail Horse

Over 100 years ago, there were only three population centres on the island: Eivissa, Sant Antoni and Santa Eulària. Sending and receiving mail was a slow process; letters were delivered on foot from the mailboat which sailed to Ibiza from Palma de Mallorca. A horse was eventually used to speed up the process but the locals were unimpressed with the innovation as the boat still never left until the evening. As a result, the mail horses were often given other, supplementary tasks like drawing water from wells.

To reach this oasis, turn right at Anita's in Sant Carles and keep following the signs to Cala Llenya. A broken sign to Cala Mastella hangs beside a dirt track, typical of the island's best out-of-the-way places. This track ends at the cove, where you can park behind the reed beds that mark the edge of the sand.

To the left, a path leads over a big pile of rocks. Follow this round to the next cove and you will come to the Don Bigote restaurant on a wooden deck, jutting out over the water on stilts. People eat at long benches and the dish of the day – the only dish – bubbles away enticingly in a pot over an open fire in the corner. Wooden fishing boats are pulled up on the beach, having brought in the catch of the day. The restaurant is extremely popular, so arrive early.

Another alternative for a long, lazy lunch in the sun is the restaurant **Sa Seni**, located behind Cala Mastella. Wooden benches and sun umbrellas are dotted around a charming rose garden and the friendly proprietress serves mouthwatering local dishes including an enormous platter of *guixat de peix* – fresh fish and potatoes cooked with saffron and spices.

Below: *Paths lead along much of Santa Eulària's rugged coastal landscape.*

Left: *The Hippodrome is an unusual attraction, drawing competitors from all over Spain.*

South from Santa Eulària

Hippodrome *

Ibiza's *Hipódromo* is situated on the road from Santa Eulària to Sant Rafel. It was constructed in 1991 and modelled on the famous La Zarzuela race course in Madrid. The stadium attracts an elegant crowd, eager for diversion between dinner and a nightclub.

Racing starts late, usually after midnight, with computerized betting and low stakes making this a cost-effective evening out for travellers on any budget. You don't even have to bet at all, but can simply soak up the glamour and excitement of the occasion. The style of racing is trotting and the idea is for the horse to pull the jockey on a lightweight chariot without breaking into a canter more than three times (this leads to disqualification). The skill is extraordinary and racers come to Ibiza from all over Spain.

Spanish Police

There are three types of police in Spain. In rural locations, the most prolific are the **Guardia Civil**, founded in 1848 to fight bandits in the countryside. Guardia Civil wear green uniforms with black tricorn hats and handle traffic offences and law and order generally. Smaller towns have a **Policia Municipal** (urban police), who wear navy blue and deal with local crimes and urban traffic control. They are funded by the Town Hall. Towns with a population of more than 20,000 also have a **Policia Nacional**, armed with machine guns and funded by the government. Policia Nacional, who wear navy blue, are responsible for dealing with serious crime on a nationwide basis.

Roca Llisa Golf *

Ibiza has two golf courses, one nine-hole and one 18-hole, spread across the hillside off the old Eivissa-Santa Eulària road. To get there, turn off towards La Siesta if coming south from Santa Eulària or take the same road, signposted Jesús, from Eivissa.

The clubhouse and pro shop are friendly and equipment can be hired. The price of a round is relatively high, although it does include as much golf as you like. Something of a blind eye is turned towards holiday

Above: *Cala Llonga, once beautiful, has unfortunately been overdeveloped.*

hackers unless the course is very busy. Generally, the scenery is very pretty as the course winds between olive groves, ploughed red-soil fields and pine trees. Not the easiest of courses, Roca Llisa has some unusual holes: at the second, for example, the tee shot is across a wide lake with a steep slope on the opposite bank. Subsequent holes cross small quarries, cultivated gardens, and fairways that are more like the rough. The views from here, however, are exhilarating, particularly when the course nears the coastline and the deep blue glint of the sea flashes enticingly in the sun.

Best Beaches for Families

The best family beaches in Ibiza and Formentera are as follows:
Platja d'en Bossa: long, sandy beach with plenty of facilities and Aquamar Park for added entertainment.
Cala Bassa: peaceful but easily reached from Sant Antoni by road or boat. Beach bars and pedalos for hire.
Es Canar: half-moon of yellow sand within walking distance of hotels. Roped off areas for safe swimming.
Cala Llonga: shallow bay close to hotels with good facilities and gentle slope for safe bathing.
Port de Sant Miquel: wide sandy beach with good facilities and safe snorkelling.

Walking around Cala Llonga **

Close to the golf course is Cala Llonga, billed as a big holiday resort but in fact rather sadly overdeveloped. What was once an attractive, deep fjord is now piled high with boxy hotel developments and international restaurants, the beach strewn with sun loungers and pedalos. White, cube-like villas, partly shaded by pine trees, look down from the hillside. The scenery around this area, however, is remarkably beautiful, and adventurous visitors can actually walk all the way to Cala Llonga from Santa Eulària. An ancient mule track crosses the two coastal mountains, **Puig d'en Pep** at 240m (785ft) and **Puig Marina** at 205m (670ft). Many of the island's hiking trails are in a state of disrepair but this one is properly waymarked with stone cairns and red paint daubed on rocks.

The coastal path from Santa Eulària starts at a large cairn on the beach south of the river mouth, just beyond the Siesta Playa hotel. Follow the trail into a shady pine wood and continue along the coast path, veering close towards the cliffs. The waymarkers are clear but additional landmarks are a villa approximately 15 minutes from the cairn and a defence tower towards the south that comes into view after 20 minutes. Walk up the track on a concrete section and follow a turn-off to the right, marked with red arrows. Now the climb begins in earnest, up through the trees and past relics of old Ibiza, such as an ancient charcoal burner. When the path forks and both directions are marked, follow the route to the left, signposted 'Llonga'. The path slopes downwards, with stunning views of the coast to the left. Eventually, you'll find yourself walking along a ridge covered with trees, before another knee-trembling descent. An asphalt road joins the trail from the right but simply continue to follow the waymarkers, passing another charcoal burner and climbing the second small mountain.

The track narrows towards the summit and along another ridge, and when it starts to descend again, you'll be fending off branches and thistles, a common feature of walking in Ibiza. Soon afterwards, about one and a half hours from the start, the path turns into a dirt road, from where you can see the hotels and beach of **Cala Llonga** and start looking forward to a cool *cerveza* (beer).

WHITEWASH

Ibiza's dazzling white, cube-like houses are carefully maintained every spring with a fresh coat of paint, usually a woman's job. A practical explanation for the white colour is that white helps to reflect the rays of the sun, keeping the interior of the building cool. Some believe, however, that the frantic painting in spring derives from an ancient Punic ritual of exorcizing darkness and therefore, evil.

Left: *Inland from Cala Llonga, ploughed red-soil fields are typical of the scenery.*

Santa Eulària at a Glance

Best Times to Visit

Santa Eulària has a permanent population and never really 'closes down' in winter. Having said this, the town is much quieter outside the months of May to October, just like the rest of the island. For nature lovers, **spring** is an ideal time to visit. The poppy fields and meadows around Sant Carles are at their most beautiful in **May**, and the first Sunday in May usually the start of the tourist season – is Santa Eulària's big flower festival with a procession of decorated floats, marching bands and several flower competitions.

Local saints' days:
Santa Eulària, 12 February; Sant Bartomeu, 24 August.

Getting There

Just 14km (9 miles) from Eivissa, Santa Eulària is accessible by **public bus** or **taxi**. Buses from Santa Eulària connect to the outlying areas of Es Canar and Sant Carles. The drive from Eivissa takes about 20 minutes, either along the main road or a twisting, scenic route through the villages of Jesús and La Siesta, passing the island's golf club.

Getting Around

Santa Eulària itself is compact and easy to **walk** around. Es Canar and the Wednesday hippie market are a 90-minute walk away across fields and country lanes, or a 15-minute bus journey. **Buses** are regular, cheap and efficient but do not run very late, stopping at around 23:00 when Eivissa is just waking up. There are **taxi ranks** in Es Canar and Santa Eulària. Boat taxis also run from Santa Eulària and Es Canar to Cala Nova and Cala Llenya north of Es Canar, and S'Argamassa and Cala Pada between Santa Eulària and Es Canar. Larger **boats** service Eivissa and Formentera.

Where to Stay

This area mainly attracts families, with a good deal of three-star-level hotel accommodation and self-catering apartments. Es Canar is very British and, compared to other resorts, fairly quiet in the evenings. Many of the hotels have children's activities and entertainment programmes.

Santa Eulària
Luxury
Hotel San Marino, Ricardo Curtoys G., Santa Eulària 1, tel: 971 33 03 16, fax: 971 33 90 76. Attractive, four-star hotel in town centre.
Hotel Fenicia, Platja dels Pins, Can Fita, tel: 971 33 01 01. Large, four-star beach hotel.
Club Punta Arabi, Apdo 73, Santa Eulària, tel: 971 33 06 50, fax: 971 33 91 67. Young people's holiday village with typical, Ibizenco villa-style accommodation. Plenty of sports, nightclubs, pools and beaches. Popular with Germans; site of weekly hippie market.

Mid-range
Hotel La Cala, c/Huesca 1, Santa Eulària, tel: 971 33 00 09, fax: 971 33 15 12. New three-star hotel with 180 rooms, located just behind the marina.

Budget
Sa Rota, c/San Vicente, tel: 971 33 00 22. Cheap *hostal* on the main nightlife street.

Es Canar
Mid-range
Hotel Anfora Playa, Platja des Canar 170, tel: 971 33 01 76, fax: 971 33 25 74. Friendly hotel in quiet area of Es Canar. Shady grounds and swimming pool a few metres from the beach.
Hotel Panorama, Platja des Canar, tel: 971 33 00 00, fax: 971 33 21 00. Es Canar's original, British-built hotel, with 137 rooms and swimming pool.

Elsewhere
Mid-range
Hotel Cala Llonga, Cala Llonga, Santa Eulària, tel: 971 19 65 01, fax: 971 19

Santa Eulària at a Glance

65 13. 300 rooms set in pine woods overlooking Cala Llonga, a quiet fjord south of Santa Eulària.
Club Can Jordi, Apdo 111, Sant Carles, tel: 971 33 51 21, fax: 971 33 53 99. Villas set in pleasant pine woods between Cala Llenya and the peaceful Cala Mastella.
Hotel Club Cala Blanca, Platja Figueral, Sant Carles, tel: 971 33 60 00. Located on quiet beach to the north of Sant Carles, near to the nudist beach.

Budget
C'an Bufí, Urb. Siesta, tel: 971 33 00 16, fax: 971 33 00 16. Pretty, 15-room *hostal* with swimming pool, run by friendly couple. Located just south of Santa Eulària.
Camping Florida, Cala Martina ap. 302, 07840 Santa Eulària, tel/ fax: 971 33 16 98. Camping in the pine woods outside Santa Eulària. Facilities include a cafeteria.

Where to Eat

Santa Eulària has some of the best restaurants on the island, mostly concentrated in the pedestrianized Carrer Sant Vicent. It is also worth exploring the outlying beaches – almost all have a *chiringuita* (a low-key restaurant serving fish and snacks).
Rincon de Pepe, Carrer Sant Vicent 53, tel: 971 33 13 21. Fantastic tapas from huge selection. Friendly service, good wine, lots of ambience.
Bar Los Amigos, Carrer Sant Vicent 28, tel: 971 31 93 59. Tiny, local bar with atmosphere, perfect for pre-dinner drinks and tapas.
Restaurante La Rambla, Passeig de S'Alamera 18, tel. 971 33 08 57. Eclectic cuisine on Santa Eulària's tiny *rambla*, including duck with blackcurrant sauce, stuffed pancakes and peppers filled with crab.
Marhaba, Carrer Sant Vicent, tel: 971 33 21 15. Moorish design with low tables and squashy cushions. Arabic *meze* a speciality.
Wild Asparagus, Cala Llonga, tel: 971 33 15 67. Countryside location outside Cala Llonga serving a variety of local dishes including grilled wild mushrooms, rabbit and monkfish in champagne.
Bar Anita, Sant Carles. Located in the centre of Sant Carles. Tapas, *hierbas*, Spanish specialities and pizza in the island's most famous hippie hangout.
Sa Seni, Cala Mastella. Idyllic lunch stop beside a deserted, beautiful beach serving *guixat de peix* in style in a pretty garden.

Tours and Excursions

Santa Eulària is well placed for exploring the northern part of the island, and for sport including golf, riding and watersports. The resort is also good for shopping, especially along the Carrer Sant Jaume and in the markets.
Hippie market: At Punta Arabi, open 10:00–19:00 on Wednesday. Walk or take the boat from Santa Eulària.
Golf: At Roca Llisa, tel: 971 19 61 18, fax: 971 31 12 20. One price covers a whole day; 27 holes.
Horse riding: Easy Rider Cala Llonga, tel: 971 19 65 11.
Craft markets: All day Saturday at Las Dalias, Sant Carles and daily except Wednesday and Sunday in the *rambla* at Santa Eulària.
There are **windsurfing** and **sailing** schools at S'Argamassa, tel: 971 33 09 19, and Santa Eulària, tel: 971 33 00 04.

Useful Contacts

Tourist office, Carrer Mariano Riquer Wallis 4, tel: 971 33 07 28, fax: 971 33 29 59.
Buses, H.F. Vilàs, tel: 971 34 03 82, website: www.ibizabus.com
Taxi rank, tel: 971 33 00 63.
Car hire, Panorama Car Hire, Es Canar, tel: 971 33 08 22.

5
The North

Ibiza's wild, rugged north is one of the most beautiful parts of the island. Just one major road winds its way over dramatic craggy hills, thick with pine woods, and passing the occasional whitewashed village nestling in a fertile valley.

There are only three holiday resorts in the north: **Cala Sant Vicent**, **Portinatx**, and **Port de Sant Miquel**. The principal village, **Sant Joan de Labritja**, is little more than a couple of streets of sleepy houses, surrounded by lush poppy fields in spring.

While there are no major tourist attractions in this part of the island, there is plenty in the way of entertainment. Ride a horse through the shade of the olive groves and juniper trees or hire a mountain bike and tackle the steep twists of the minor roads. From Portinatx, hire a boat and explore some of the island's most remote, inaccessible beaches. There are plenty of vigorous hikes along the coast or alternatively, countless excellent fish restaurants situated right on the beach where you can happily spend several hours mellowing out.

Don't Miss

*** **Portinatx:** known for its pretty bays.
*** **Hiking:** the area around Sant Miquel offers several options.
** **Folk dancing and craft market:** two of Sant Miquel's major attractions.
** **Balafi:** the island's only remaining Moorish village.
* **Art galleries:** discover local artists in Santa Gertrudis.

Cala Sant Vicent *

Once a remote fjord and now a busy holiday resort, Cala Sant Vicent is located in the far northeast of Ibiza. A wide swathe of off-white sand with cliffs at either end is lined with hotels and apartment blocks. There are plenty of facilities here, from beach volleyball to mini-golf. Boats make daytrips to the island of **Tagomago**, an uninhabited chunk of rock rising 100m (330ft) above sea level and

Opposite: *Most rugged of Ibiza's coasts, the north is extraordinarily beautiful.*

> **NATURISM**
>
> Ibiza has a relaxed attitude to nude sunbathing and a few beaches have been designated 'official'. These are **S'Aigua Blanca** in the northeast and **Platja de Ses Salines** (at the northern end) and **Platja d'Es Cavallet** in the south. Es Cavallet is predominantly gay. Topless sunbathing is acceptable elsewhere but do dress with respect in the villages, where old people retain traditional, more conservative values.

crowned by a lighthouse. There are a couple of little *calas* where yachts moor for a picnic and the island is a good place on which to spot the rare Eleanora's falcon or watch glossy black cormorants diving for fish. Boats also run from Sant Vicent to the beaches of **Es Figueral** and **Pou des Lleó** to the south, for a change of scene.

Es Cuieram **

Hidden in the hills above Cala Sant Vicent is one of the island's most important archaeological discoveries, the cave of **Es Cuieram**, a shrine dedicated to the goddess **Tanit** from 4–2BC.

While there is little to see today, the story of the cave is nonetheless fascinating. Hundreds of gold medallions and terracotta figures were discovered here in 1907, although many more were probably stolen earlier by Arab pirates who plundered the old Punic sites of worship. Some of the 20th-century finds are in the museum at Puig des Molins in Eivissa but many that were discovered had been blackened by fire, suggesting that some kind of funerary ceremonies were held in the cave. In 1929 another exciting discovery was made – a bronze plaque, over 2000 years old, referring to Tanit herself. The walk up to the cave is a rough one, through dense undergrowth and over rocks, but worth the effort.

PORTINATX ★★★

The main resort on the north coast, Portinatx, has two claims to fame. In 1929, the then tiny port received a royal visit from **King Alfonso XIII** and promptly rechristened itself 'Portinatx del Rey' ('of the King'). There was further upheaval in the village several years later when some scenes from the film *South Pacific* were shot here, a fact on which several bars and restaurants continue to trade.

The yellow cliffs and typically Mediterranean scenery of silvery olives and scrubby gorse and thyme do not evoke images of the Pacific until you see the water at Portinatx, where it is an incredible shade of aquamarine, fading into deep sapphire out to sea. No wonder some of Ibiza's most wealthy immigrants have built houses here.

The village itself is nothing special architecturally, just a straggle of low-rise, whitewashed hotels and the usual colourful jumble of plastic airbeds, souvenir T-shirts and postcards lining the streets. There are, however, three beautiful sandy beaches. The best one is right at the far end of the village, where fishing boats are pulled up on a narrow spit of sand leading to several large flat rocks, perfect for sunbathing. From here, the coast continues round to the east in a series of impressive sandstone cliffs, guarded by a lighthouse. At the restaurant **Cas Mallorquí** you can look down from the

TAX-FREE SHOPPING

Visitors to Spain who are not European Union (EU) residents can claim a refund of Spanish value added tax (IVA), currently at 16%. Purchases must exceed 15,000 pesetas per item and must be exported within three months of purchase. Look for the tax-free signs in shops and ask the assistant for a tax-free shopping cheque. This should be stamped by customs when you leave the EU. After customs, the airport has a refund point where you can get your money back. There are also refund offices in most other European airports, should you be touring around.

Opposite: *Sant Joan de Labritja, the north's principal village, has a fine church.*
Above: *The off-white sand of Cala Sant Vicent, lined with hotels and apartments.*

terrace into the clear water. Fresh fish is brought out from the kitchen on a platter so guests can choose their lunch and after the meal, *hierbas*, the house speciality, is produced – a big bottle crammed with sprigs of rosemary, juniper berries and some unidentifiable leaves, marinating in anise to create a medicinal-tasting but interesting digestif.

Car Hire

There are plenty of car hire companies on Ibiza and Formentera, with anything from air-conditioned automatics to open-top jeeps on offer. You will need an international driving permit (or a pink licence if you are from an EC country). Most companies ask for a deposit, so paying by credit card is preferable. Petrol stations are plentiful in Ibiza, although Formentera has only one, which closes in the evenings. It is not worth taking a car on the ferry to Formentera for a daytrip; hire bicycles instead. While crime is minimal on both islands, take care not to leave valuables in the car.

Cala d'en Serra **

Accessible via a steep dirt track from the main road to Portinatx or, more interestingly, by motorboat from the beach in Portinatx, this exquisite cove represents some of Ibiza's wildest and most untouched scenery.

The *cala* is a deep coastal inlet, hollowed out by the waves to form a semicircle of coarse, white sand strewn with rounded boulders. Steep cliffs at either side are covered with pine and juniper trees, although there is no shade on the beach itself. Clusters of rocks underwater make this a wonderful place for leisurely and exploratory snorkelling. Refreshments are provided by only one tiny beach bar at Cala d'en Serra.

Cala Xuclar

Heading in the opposite direction from Portinatx, this once-pretty beach is now a sorry scene of neglect. Deserted and rather dirty, junk is piled up on the sand and there are great heaps of black seaweed at the water's edge.

Cala Xarraca **

In complete contrast, this stunning cove off the main Portinatx road is perfect for a long lunch at the restaurant there, followed by an afternoon spent basking on the warm rocks. A sheltered inlet protected from sea winds by low-lying cliffs, **Cala Xarraca**, with its rocky sea floor, is ideal for snorkellers. A tiny island guards the entrance to the cove. Pedalos are available for hire on the beach and you can quite safely potter around the rocky **Punta de Xarraca** headland.

Opposite: *Nothing special architecturally, Portinatx is nonetheless full of colour.*
Below: *The quaint cove of Cala Xaracca has a rocky sea floor, wonderful for snorkelling.*

Hiking around Portinatx

There are some challenging walks around the Portinatx area. One is the 10km (6-mile) hike from Punta de Xarraca to Cala Portinatx which crosses some fairly rough country along the coastline. Also worth trying if you're fit is the 11km (7-mile) trail from Sant Joan to Portinatx. This route follows an old bridle path once used, before the advent of the car, by locals in Portinatx as the main route to Sant Joan. The trail follows the line of several beautiful valleys and is particularly pretty in spring. However, be careful walking inland between July and August: without a cooling sea breeze, temperatures can be uncomfortable.

A Tasty Treat

Cheese from neighbouring Menorca is often served on Ibiza as a dessert. Soft rain and light humidity create Menorca's green pastures, an ideal environment in which to raise dairy herds. It is these conditions which have produced the delicious cheese first recorded in the 5th century AD.
The cheese is made by *madones* – country women who retain old-fashioned production methods and formulas, which include hanging the cheese by grass ropes to cure. The flavour is strong and aromatic; young cheeses are creamy, hardening to taste more like English cheddar after a few weeks and eventually attaining the crumbly texture of parmesan. Formentera also makes rather pungent cheese from goat or sheep's milk, available in shops in Sant Ferran and Sant Francesc.

Sant Miquel de Balansat ***

If there is a 'typical' Ibizenco village anywhere on the island, Sant Miquel is it. High in **Els Amunts**, Ibiza's mountain range, the whitewashed village is surrounded by thick pine forests interspersed with cultivated fields and citrus groves, all neatly divided up by low stone walls.

Sant Miquel's church was one of the first to be built on the island and part of its walls date back to the 14th century. The remainder was built in 1690 and has a hint of Italian Baroque style. Like many Ibizenco churches, the building resembles a small fortress, and like other villages, Sant Miquel itself is built some distance from its port as a means of protection from pirate raids.

Despite the tourist coaches that trundle through the sleepy village, Sant Miquel has kept a firm grip on traditional culture. Every Thursday at 18:00 there's a display of traditional *ball pagés*, or country dancing, opposite the church, after which *hierbas* is passed around. The dancing comes complete with a compere and an explanation of the moves in four languages.

Port de Sant Miquel *

This once-beautiful cove is now something of a disappointment thanks to excessive development. A huge hotel and apartment complex clings to a wooded hillside, putting a great deal of pressure on the tiny beach below in peak season. If you drive up the cliff road behind the hotels, however, the view down over the buildings is of dramatic cliffs, rocky offshore islands and deep blue sea, with perhaps a couple of yachts bobbing in the bay. Outside July and August this is a popular spot among sailors mooring up for lunch and a swim.

Left: *Pine woods cover the headland of Port de Sant Miquel.*
Opposite: *Whitewashed architecture in Sant Miquel makes it one of the island's most characteristic villages.*

On a rocky spit of land, colonies of seagulls breed around the **Torre del Mutar** watchtower, which guards the entrance to the inlet. Before the hotels were built, the villagers would celebrate their saint's day on 29 September with feasting in the port.

On the same cliff road are the **Coves de Ca Na Marça**, natural limestone caves which have been illuminated to create a sound and light show. Open 10:00–18:00 daily.

Continue from here to the exquisite **Cala de Benirras** where sheer cliffs fall away into the blue and a tiny, rock-strewn beach is a good spot from which to swim and snorkel. Hippies bang bongo drums here at sunset and hold regular full moon parties.

Hotel Hacienda ★★

In the pine woods on the headland to the south of Port de Sant Miquel, the island's most exclusive hotel provides an oasis of luxurious calm. The restaurant is open to nonresidents and when there's a buffet round the lagoon-like pool at lunchtime, visitors can have a swim as well. The hotel is a member of the Relais et Chateaux group and, if you can afford it, perfect for a romantic getaway.

Birds of Prey

Anyone hiking along the remote coasts of Ibiza and Formentera will spot birds of prey wheeling high in the sky. Kestrels and ravens are familiar sights and occasionally visitors will spot the large wingspan of the Eleanora's falcon, a large bird which breeds on the rocky, offshore islets and in the high cliffs. The falcons are migratory and arrive in the Balearics in April, when they can be spotted hunting large beetles over Ses Salines. The Eleanora's falcon is endangered and the Balearic population represents a significant chunk of the world's remaining colonies.
A rare sight is the booted eagle, which lives in the high, remote hills of the north and raids farms occasionally at lambing time.

Right: *The Hotel Hacienda commands stunning views over the sea.*
Opposite: *Scenes of rural life abound around the inland village of Sant Miquel.*

How to be a Green Visitor

The tourism industry is becoming increasingly environmentally conscious and individual visitors can contribute to protecting Ibiza and Formentera's fragile ecosystems.

- Never leave litter lying around.
- Don't buy souvenirs made of shells.
- Don't take shells from the sea.
- Do not create a demand for things like lobster when they are out of season.
- Hire a bicycle instead of a car.
- Do not use jetskis or create water, air or noise pollution.
- Choose a tour operator that is committed to protecting the environment.
- Choose a hotel which has a responsible attitude to conservation, i.e. water recycling.

Hiking around Sant Miquel ***

Hike round the headland of **Punta de sa Creu**, from outside Sant Miquel village to the beach. The walk, through stunningly beautiful coastal scenery and open meadows, takes a couple of hours.

Turn off the main road from Sant Miquel to the port just after the small river bridge. Here a track heads uphill to the left. Walk past overgrown orchards and gardens, divided by crumbling, low stone walls. Gnarled olive trees, carob and big clusters of prickly pear grow here. After about 20 minutes, you'll come to a whitewashed, walled-in well on the left. Before houses had plumbing, these wells were the focal point of village life. While the whitewash on this one is dazzling, the water inside is full of frogs!

Turn left after the well and go past some houses on the right and a small sand quarry and a water tank on the left. The views are spectacular; mile after mile of rolling, pine-clad hills with no sign of civilization except for the odd, lonely farmhouse. Whenever the path forks, keep to the left; a deep valley will be on your right as the trail climbs. Before passing into a pine wood, you will see some waymarkers on a stone although, typical of Ibizenco hikes, these do not reappear to show the way further on.

After about 40 minutes (from the start of the hike), the sea comes into view through the pines. The trail continues to twist and turn, while now following the coastline, offering incredible views of a spectacular bay, completely deserted because of the sheer cliffs protecting it. Sometimes, a lone yacht will moor here for a private on-board picnic.

Around another corner, the sprawling white cubes and pool of the Hotel Hacienda come into view below the trail. Next you will see the asphalt road that leads to the hotel. Turn right here, away from the hotel, and head down the hill. If you see names daubed in fading paint across the road, this is not an example of Ibizenco graffiti, but of the tradition during a big cycle race to write the name of one's hero across the road. Like the rest of Spain, Ibiza is cycling-mad.

Follow the road down through shady, deciduous forest with a dried-up riverbed to the left. Again, disused gardens and orchards lie below and out of the wood; there are some spectacularly large fig trees growing in a meadow, so vast that their branches are supported by smaller trees. The meadows are a blaze of colour in spring.

Eventually, the route joins the main road again and the beach and holiday apartments of Port Sant Miquel come into view.

An alternative walk is east from Port de Sant Miquel to Cala de Benirras. The path descends into Cova d'en Marcà, ideal for a swimming stop.

Forgotten Wells

Ancient disused wells are scattered all over Ibiza and give a good indication of places which once would have been used for social gatherings. You can often spot a well in a field by looking for a cluster of prickly pears around a pile of rubble. Cisterns and tanks are still used for storing water, all of which comes from underground sources, but the pumps nowadays are electric and the windmills, sadly, no longer used.

The Porron

At barbecue evenings or gatherings in the country, you'll see local people drinking from the *porron*, a strange-looking vessel that resembles a watering can with a wide mouth and long, pointed spout. The idea is to tip the *porron* and drink without touching it, in accordance, legend has it, with a Muslim premise that wine must never touch the lips. Using a *porron* with the right kind of flourish is not easy and when one is experimenting with sangria on a hot summer's night, it's possible to consume huge amounts without noticing…

DONKEY TREKS

Donkeys have become something of a parody in Ibiza, having survived as a beast of burden for centuries. The sight of a farmer on a donkey laden with straw baskets is a very rare one now but just outside Santa Gertrudis, a *burro* ranch recreates everything for the sake of the visitor. A night out here involves a 20-minute trek by donkey over the hills, followed by copious drinking from a *porron.*

Opposite top: *Stone walls are a common countryside feature.*
Opposite bottom: *The small village of Sant Mateu lies beside a gentle range of hills.*
Below: *Outside Santa Gertrudis de Fruitera, locals gather potatoes.*

Inland Villages

Balafi ★

Off the main road from Portinatx to Eivissa, just before the hamlet of **Sant Llorenc** is the tiny, easily missed village of Balafi. To get there, look for a sign on the right, almost buried in the undergrowth, and bump up a dirt track heading south.

Balafi is unusual in that it is the island's only village surviving from Moorish times, 1000 years ago. The name 'Balafi' is Arabic (almost every other village in Ibiza is named after a Christian saint) and the architecture is typical of the time. The town is a cluster of white flat-roofed houses – the alleys between them just wide enough for a donkey – and a collection of rounded stone towers which would have formed the last line of defence if marauding pirates had reached this far inland.

Sant Llorenc itself is a typically sleepy country village set around a pretty church. On 10 August, the saint's day *ball pagés* (traditional dances) are performed here.

Santa Gertrudis de Fruitera ★

This hamlet is certainly worth a stop on a round-the-island drive. What looks at first like a typical white village dozing in the hot sun turns out to be a thriving centre of art and culture. There are two good galleries in the village, **Punta A** and **Can Daita**, and two more just to the south, **Elefante** and **Es Moli**. The bar **Can Costa** is famous as a gathering place for both locals and the island's expatriate artistic community and you can usually eavesdrop or join in with good conversation.

Between Santa Gertrudis and Sant Rafel is the Hippodrome riding stable. Rides out into the country can be arranged as well as excursions in a horse-drawn carriage accompanied by a driver.

Forest Fires

Forest fires are a serious threat to Ibiza in summer when the undergrowth becomes dry and brittle. Visitors should observe a strict code of conduct:

- Never light fires in the wild if a sign forbids it, or throw away cigarette butts or leave glass objects lying around.
- Where campfires are permitted, put them out with water and earth and make sure there are no embers still glowing when you leave.
- If you see a fire, please report it immediately.

Calas of the North ***

The remainder of the northwest coast from **Port de Sant Miquel** to **Cala Salada**, just north of Sant Antoni, represents Ibiza's wildest and most inaccessible area. A rough dirt track runs across the mountains from the tiny village of **Sant Mateu** to the exquisite **Cala d'Eubarca**, accessed only by a steep, twisting path through the trees. The shoreline at the base of the cliffs is rocky with steep underwater drop-offs, giving the sea a deep indigo colour. This remote spot is rarely crowded; in fact, for most of the year, nobody comes here at all.

If you choose to hike, wear good boots and carry water and a compass. There are some good picnic spots amongst the pine trees on top of the cliffs with tantalizing views of the Mediterranean below. A rather more hedonistic way to explore this beautiful yet inhospitable coastline is by yacht or speedboat. Some of the coves are not suitable for landing but you can drop anchor and swim from the boat.

The North at a Glance

Best Times to Visit

Out of season, this part of the island is very, very quiet. **Spring**, with the countryside in blossom, is a beautiful time to travel and the best time for enjoying the superb hiking in this area. In **winter**, however, the resorts all but close up.

Local saints' days:
Sant Joan, 24 June;
Santa Maria, 5 August.

Getting There

Buses run from Eivissa to Portinatx, but only about five times a day.

Taxis will make the 30km (20-mile) journey but the fare is high as the road is full of hairpin bends towards the north and the trip takes some time. Likewise for the two other main resorts in this region, Port Sant Miquel and Cala Sant Vicent.

Getting Around

Car rental is strongly recommended when staying in the north of Ibiza. Bus services are scant. If you want to explore, a car will probably end up cheaper than a series of taxis. Cycling enthusiasts should consider hiring a **bicycle**. The hilly countryside makes for a challenging holiday but the roads are quiet up here and the scenery stunning. There is also some superb **hiking** country in the area; for real, off the beaten track excursions, remember to bring a compass.

Where to Stay

Accommodation is concentrated around Cala Sant Vicent, Portinatx and Port Sant Miquel. While the municipality is named after Sant Joan, the capital itself is no more than a tiny, sleepy village. Several of the hotels are in 'vacation club' style and offer a daily programme of organized activities.

Luxury

Hotel Hacienda, Aptdo 423 Ibiza, tel: 971 33 45 00, fax: 971 33 45 14. The island's most exclusive hotel, part of the Relais et Chateaux group, located on a cliff at Na Xamena outside Sant Miquel. There are 65 luxurious rooms, restaurant, tennis court and three pools.

Hacienda Encanto del Rio, Aptdo 197, Sant Carles, tel: 971 33 50 34, fax: 971 33 51 52. Small, deluxe villa in pine woods near Agua Blanca beach, owned by Swiss footballer Heinz Hermann. Nine apartments and one villa.

Residence Can Talaias, Sant Carles. Tranquil hilltop retreat north of Sant Carles, with just six rooms in the house owned by the late actor Terry Thomas.

Mid-range

Hotel Cala San Vicente, Cala Sant Vicent, tel: 971 33 20 21, fax: 971 33 33 44. Modern three-star on quiet beach in a beautiful cove.

Hotel Imperio Playa, Cala Sant Vicent, tel: 971 33 30 55. 210-room three-star hotel.

Hotel El Greco, Cala Portinatx, tel: 971 33 30 48. Large three-star hotel with plenty of facilities.

Es Pujolel, Santa Agnes – Sant Mateu Road, tel: 971 80 51 70. Very quiet location. Homemade food.

Club Portinatx, Platja de Portinatx, tel: 971 33 30 77. Holiday club with lively atmosphere, nightclub, plenty of sporting activities and small beach at the base of the cliffs.

Hotel Cartago, Port de Sant Miquel, tel: 971 33 45 51, fax: 971 33 45 32. Large, three-star port hotel.

Hotel Galeón, Port de Sant Miquel, tel: 971 33 45 34. Lively hotel with 182 rooms in beautiful, mountainside setting overlooking the beach.

Budget

Apartamentos Balansat, Port de Sant Miquel, tel/fax: 971 33 45 37. Simple apartments right on the beach in pretty Port de Sant Miquel.

Cas Mallorquí, Portinatx, tel: 971 33 30 67, fax: 971 33 31 59. Hotel/restaurant on the beach. Simple accommodation in 11 rooms.

The North at a Glance

Where to Eat

Hostal Des Arcades, Crtra Sant Joan km20, tel: 971 33 30 02, fax: 971 33 31 70. Small *hostal* located between Eivissa and Sant Joan.

La Plaza, Plaça de la Iglesia, Santa Gertrudis, tel: 971 19 70 75. French cuisine in attractive garden setting.

Es Caliu, on the Sant Joan-Eivissa road km10, tel: 971 32 50 75. Spanish specialities in a country restaurant.

Cana Pepeta, Carretera Eivissa–Portinatx km14.4, tel: 971 32 50 23. Ibizenco specialities served on a comfortable shady terrace.

Bar Costa, Plaça de la Iglesia, Santa Gertrudis, tel: 971 19 70 21. Atmospheric snack bar in the village square.

C'an Gall, Carretera Eivissa–Sant Joan km12.3, tel: 971 33 29 16. Converted farmhouse serving local specialities. Good wine list.

Cas Mallorquí, Portinatx, tel: 971 33 30 67. Friendly restaurant with big terrace overlooking the water. Fresh fish and paella specialities. Be sure to try the homemade *hierbas*.

Tours and Excursions

Essentially, this part of the island is very quiet and attracts people who are either interested in hiking and cycling or are looking for a peaceful beach holiday. Nightlife is limited and you'll often have to drive or take a taxi to a good restaurant. Buses run to Eivissa, but in the evening, you'll need to get a taxi back.

The main line serving Sant Miquel is **Autocares Lucas Costa**, tel: 971 31 27 55, while **Francisco Vilàs S.A.**, tel: 971 31 16 01, operates services to Sant Joan, Cala Sant Vicent and Portinatx.

Tour operators run round-the-island tours, picking up guests in the various resorts; these can be booked locally. There are, however, no public excursions in the north.

In Cala Sant Vicent, visit the Punic sanctuary **Es Cuieram** above the resort, reached by a steep path. In Sant Miquel (the village, not the port) there is traditional **country dancing** outside the church every Thursday at 18:15.

Boats can be hired at Port de Sant Miquel, Portinatx and Cala Sant Vicent for trips to neighbouring bays. There is a **windsurfing** school at Portinatx.

Scuba diving: Subfari, Cala Portinatx, tel: 971 33 31 83, or San Miquel, Port de Sant Miquel, tel: 971 33 45 39.

Walking: Ask at the tourist board in Eivissa (situated at Passeig Vara del Rey) about special hiking leaflets for the northern region. There are three or four good, fairly testing hikes for which you will need specific directions and a map.

Riding: Club Campo de Caballo, Santa Getrudis, tel: 649 45 77 18.

Useful Contacts

Police, Carrer Principal, tel: 971 33 30 35.

Post Office, Carretera Sant Joan, km 21.

Ajuntament (Town Hall) of Sant Joan, tel: 971 33 30 03.

6
The South

Visitors can find plenty to explore in Ibiza's southern region and the scenery provides some vivid contrasts; the islet of **Es Vedrà** appears as a ghostly pinnacle while the saltpans at **Ses Salines** shimmer in a heat-induced haze. The landscape rises up to the island's highest peak, **Sa Talaiassa**, south of the village of **Sant Josép**, and falls away in a series of steep cliffs and rounded coves all the way around the south coast. The pine-clad hills flatten out into a plain, now heavily farmed, in the southeast, where Eivissa has spread its tentacles along the wide, sandy beaches. The island's southernmost point, however, is unspoiled and undeveloped, thus offering fine walks through pine woods and over dunes to huge swathes of sand and flat rocks with breathtaking views across to the nearby island of Formentera.

There are not many holiday resorts in Ibiza's south. A few hotels and apartments line the coast at **Cala Vedella** and **Es Cubells**, but the rocky landscape has hindered much serious development. Most of the beaches, as a result, are rarely crowded and are usually frequented only by people who arrive by car or on yachts. High in the hills, exclusive villas surrounded by tropical gardens perch among the trees. Dusty country lanes meander through tiny villages with occasional views from the hilltops across the island to the white tower blocks of **Sant Antoni** in the west and the distinctive walls of Eivissa in the east – a reminder of just how small Ibiza really is.

Don't Miss

*** **Ses Salines:** dramatic salt flats and sandy beach.
** **Torre d'en Pirata:** offers spectacular views of Es Vedrà.
** **Cala d'Hort:** perfect place for Sunday lunch on the beach, Ibiza-style.
* **Sa Talaiassa:** hike up Ibiza's highest peak.
* **Es Cavallet:** vast expanse of pristine beach.

Opposite: *Cala Vedella is one of few resorts on the mainly rocky south coast.*

Sant Josép de Sa Talaia ★★

The island's largest municipality is named after this tiny, unprepossessing village perched on the slope of **Sa Talaiassa**, Ibiza's highest peak at 475m (1558ft) above sea level. The village itself is pretty enough, with several shops selling locally made lace and handicrafts. Stop and look at the **church**, built in 1726. Rather lavish for such a tiny village, the church has an interesting retable (ornamental screen) and painted stuccos, believed to have been made by a master of the time specializing in Venetian Baroque. It is always open to visitors.

Climbing Sa Talaiassa ★★

Keen walkers will enjoy the two-hour hike around the wooded peak. The views are breathtaking and the temperature slightly cooler up here, although the walk is quite tough. Good hiking boots and plenty of water are recommended.

Start the walk in Sant Josép; Sa Talaiassa is well signposted and a trail leads past village gardens to the pine woods. Two radio transmitters mark the peak, reached by a rocky path cut into steps on the steeper sections.

On Two Wheels

Bicycle and motorbike hire is a popular way to explore Ibiza and Formentera. If you are hiring a bicycle and plan to be remotely adventurous, go for a mountain bike as most of the really picturesque places are only accessible by dirt track.

A driving licence is required to hire even the most basic of motorbikes and the use of a crash helmet is compulsory. Even if you see locals and other travellers riding bareheaded, don't take the risk. You may be stopped or, worse still, injured.

Wild thyme and rosemary scent the air and brilliantly coloured butterflies flit from one flower to another in the heat. You'll spot the occasional disused charcoal burner, dating back to when charcoal provided a source of income to impoverished Ibizencos.

Just beyond the peak, the trail heads along a ridge with stunning views of the offshore islands of **Es Vedrà** and **Es Vedranell**. The cliffs of Formentera are easy to spot in the distance and on a clear day with no haze, it is possible to see the island of Mallorca. Some people claim to be able to spot the Spanish mainland but this is a rather fanciful notion and you'll need binoculars.

Around a corner, **Sant Antoni** comes into view and there are some lovely picnic spots looking down over the bay from the shade of the pine trees. The path eventually heads down to an asphalt road past heather, bright green carob trees, and juniper. Turn right on to the road and follow it back to Sant Josép.

Above: *Debating in a health shop in the village of Sant Josép de Sa Talaia.*
Below: *Though hilly, Ibiza doesn't get any higher than Sa Talaiassa at 475m (1558ft).*

Around Sant Josép

Just north of Sant Josép is the pretty village of **Sant Agustí**, built around a square-shaped church. The doors are only unlocked sporadically, but if you can get inside, you will find a Baroque altar and attractive blue and white tiles on the walls of the sanctuary.

While visiting Sant Agustí, call in at **Can Berri**, a popular bar / restaurant in an old Spanish house with chairs and tables outside.

Safe Walking

- Never light fires or throw cigarette butts on the ground – forest fires are a real danger.
- Close gates in the countryside – they are placed there for a reason.
- Always tell someone where you are going and when you expect to be back. Some of the walks on Ibiza are quite remote and people have twisted ankles and fallen into ravines in the past.
- Always carry water. Hiking in the sun is extremely dehydrating.
- Don't pick fruit or flowers – you're not in your own garden.

ISLAND PLANTS

Most things that grow on Ibiza and Formentera have a use, even if they are wild. Almonds are exported in small quantities to the mainland, while figs are consumed locally and the skins fed to farm animals. The fruits of the bright green carob trees, long dangling pods, are used as cattle feed although carob can be made into an alternative to chocolate. Prickly pears, which often grow around wells, bear edible fruit in October. You'll see them piled up in the markets. Wild herbs – particularly garlic, thyme and rosemary – are used for cooking.

The Southwest Coast

Cala Tarida ★★

A necklace of sheltered coves encircles this part of the coast, which is quiet and peaceful for much of the year. **Cala Tarida**, a well-equipped beach, is located just 6km (4 miles) west from Sant Josép and is only a short cycle ride down a winding road from the main Sant Josép–Sant Antoni road. The beach is served by bus in summer. Flat rocks shaped by wind and sea form natural platforms for sunbathing at either end of the beach, which is composed of soft white sand. The water is shallow, ideal for children, and there are sailing boats and pedalos for hire as well as a couple of good beach restaurants. Boats call in from Sant Antoni, bringing crowds of sun-worshippers, but there is usually somewhere with a bit of space.

Cala Vedella ★

This deep, almost enclosed inlet, south of Cala Tarida, looks like something out of the Caribbean with powdery white sand and warm turquoise water. The water is shallow for a fairly long way out and is thus safe for children as well as pleasantly warm from early in the season until late September.

Cala Vedella has been developed for tourism and is busy in July and August. The holiday complex here was modelled on a Spanish village and consists of white- and ochre-coloured houses with shaded balconies and patios, nestling among the pines. The complex has a swimming pool and restaurant, and all sorts of sporting activities are on offer.

For a more tranquil day spent on the beach, walk northwards along the asphalt road for a couple of kilometres to **Cala Molí**, a near-perfect little crescent of sand with steep cliffs at either side. Pine woods reach right down to the sand and provide welcome shade during the heat of the day. There's a beach bar and pedalo hire but little else apart from some villas on the hill, and the beach is rarely busy. The varying sea floor, with stretches of open sand as well as rocks, makes this a good spot for snorkelling, with colourful fish and octopus living between the fronds of seaweed and scattered boulders.

Above: *Unusual Es Vedrà is clearly visible from the quiet cove of Cala d'Hort.* **Opposite:** *Soft white sand at Cala Tarida, a short cycle ride from the main road.*

Cala Carbó ★

Another charming spot for sunbathing in relative peace and quiet is **Cala Carbó**, located between Cala Vedella and Cala d'Hort. Very little is on offer here – a short half-moon of coarse yellow sand and one simple beach restaurant – but the absence of a bus service to this cove means that it is rarely crowded. Bathing is safe and the rocky cliffs on either side protect the cove from the wind. However, there's no shade so be careful with children during the heat of the day.

Cala d'Hort ★★

The dramatic rock faces of **Es Vedrà** are visible from all around the southwest coast, but the best place from which to admire the view is at the secluded cove of **Cala d'Hort**. A bumpy road heads steeply down past a few houses to an enclosed bay of fine sand with a row of rickety boatsheds along one side. Es Vedrà, practically oozing menace and mystery, looms in front. Probably the most photographed rock around Ibiza, the island is captivating at any time of day – shrouded in mist in the early morning or silhouetted against the setting sun.

A good reason for visiting Cala d'Hort, particularly in the low season, is for Sunday lunch. Locals, usually in big

Es Vedrà

The barren rock of Es Vedrà is, like many things on Ibiza, supposed to have magical powers. A priest who went there to meditate allegedly witnessed the appearance of angels, devils and the Holy Virgin. UFOs have been sighted and fishermen have reported strange circles of light in the sea. Enthusiasts say the triangular, almost pyramid-like, shape of the rock resembles a giant channel of energy to attract UFOs.

Above: *Rocky cliffs beyond Cala d'Hort are home to rare Eleanora's falcons.*
Opposite: *An air of luxurious calm characterizes remote Es Cubells.*

noisy groups, flock to the restaurant here – the terrace of which juts out over the sand – and consume giant paellas, fragrant with saffron, and large jugs of *sangrìa*. Lunch starts at 14:00 and continues until the shadows are lengthening on the sand.

A colony of rare **Eleanora's falcons** inhabits the rocky cliff faces around Cala d'Hort. If you look carefully as they wheel high in the sky, you will be able to distinguish them from the seagulls by their broad wingspan.

Torre d'en Pirata ★

To walk off lunch, you can make the climb to an old watchtower just south of Cala d'Hort, which is reached by a steep rocky path. Signposted simply 'Torre', a dirt track turns off the main road from Cala d'Hort to Sant Josép. Park here and scramble up the hillside to the tower. The climb is very steep, past gorse and heather and over boulders. The tower itself, in a remarkable state of preservation, is built on a sheer section of cliff so be careful when walking around as it's a long way down to the piled-up rocks!

There is nothing inside the tower – just the usual litter and graffiti – but its solid stone walls and narrow window slits easily give you an impression of what it must have been like to watch for enemy sails on the horizon. This watchtower, like the many other *atalayas* (or *talaias* in Catalan), was built in the 16th century, a time when the island was particularly prone to pirate invasions. The towers, which guard the most exposed areas of the coastline, were manned constantly and were located close enough together for an early warning system to operate as soon as pirates were spotted. Fires were built on the roof or flares set off, giving the villagers time to reach the parish church or the windowless, fortified towers located throughout the island's interior.

Photography

Ibiza and Formentera are a photographer's dream, with stunning landscapes and beautiful coastal scenery. Early morning and 'magic hour' – the hour before sunset – are the best times to take pictures as the light at midday is too bright. International brands of film are available all over Ibiza and in the larger villages of Formentera. Try to avoid using film from souvenir stands, however, as it will probably have been subjected to prolonged heat and may not be of the best quality. Both 24- and 48-hour printing services are available in Ibiza and there are photographic shops in Eivissa, should a camera need repairing.

Es Cubells ★★

This is one of the quietest and most remote spots on Ibiza, a tiny village straggling along the clifftop. Several luxury villas have been built up here to take advantage of the sea views and the beauty of the rural landscape. In the village, a steep road leads down to a long narrow beach of rocks and sand. There's some good snorkelling over the rocks further out and a beach bar, but the rather deep water makes this beach less suitable for young children.

Cova Santa ★

On the right-hand side of the main road back towards Eivissa is a small cave which is open to the public. Nobody knows from where **Cova Santa** takes its name and there's not much to see, but it is nonetheless pretty with its stalactites and stalagmites.

> **ENVIRONMENTAL ISSUES**
>
> **Ses Salines** and the mountainous area of **Els Amunts** in the north are loosely protected by the Law of Natural Spaces, which limits construction in ecologically sensitive areas. Cycle paths along many of the island roads encourage visitors not to use cars. There are, however, many more unresolved issues, not least of which is preventing the local extinction of any more sea creatures like the turtles and seals that once inhabited Ibizenco waters.

Sa Caleta ★

Although there is little left today, the headland of **Mola de Sa Caleta** was one of the most important Phoenician settlements in Ibiza in the 7th century BC. The excavations are signposted from the road and can be visited.

The area was settled because of its use as a safe haven for ships, and it is believed that several hundred people lived here at one time. Evidence has been found of fishing, bread baking and weaving, as well as metallurgy furnaces for making instruments with ores brought over from the mainland. People lived in stone houses grouped into arrangements with a small square in the middle of each cluster, usually the location of a bread-baking oven. Architects believe, however, that Sa Caleta was only inhabited for about 40 years, its inhabitants moving peacefully to the settlement at Eivissa when the latter became a more important port.

The Far South ★★★

Ibiza's far southeast tip has two distinguishing features: long sandy beaches (where anything goes) and some 40.5ha (1000 acres) of **saltpans**. The saltpans are awe-inspiring to look at: shimmering lakes divided by low walls with a layer of white crystals at the bottom glittering in the sun. The road to get to the beaches of Ses Salines or Es Cavallet runs right alongside the saltpans, and the temptation to stop and take photographs is strong, particularly at sunset when the sky is streaked with crimson.

Salt has played a significant role in Ibiza's past. The island was an important stop on all the Mediterranean trading routes because salt had to be used to preserve food for long sea voyages. It was from the sale of salt that the walls around Dalt Vila were paid for. At the time the walls were constructed, in 1554, all Ibizencos owned a share in the salt industry and received free salt themselves. The workers in the saltpans were either criminals or captured pirates. The *salines* were, however, lost after the War of Spanish Succession in 1715, when the State seized them as a means of punishing Ibiza for rebelling. Islanders continued to receive free salt, but in the middle of the last century the saltpans were sold to a private company, so even this small privilege was lost. Today, some 60,000 tonnes are harvested a year and salt is the only industry, apart from tourism, from which Ibiza makes a profit.

Salt Extraction

Extracting salt is an almost entirely natural process. Two electric pumps allow sea water to flood into the saltpans but the water is then left alone to evaporate, a process which takes three months. The lumps of salt crystal are broken up and stored in huge heaps before a conveyor belt takes them to waiting container ships. Only 20 people work now in what was never a popular career. If an Ibizenco wishes an enemy ill, he will say: 'Go and haul salt'.

Above: *Salt production continues apace today, though mainland sources are increasing in volume.*
Right: *White crystals may be seen glittering at the bottom of the extensive saltpans.*

Left: *Platja de Ses Salines boasts good facilities, including this beach bar.*

Beaches ★★★

The two long sandy beaches in the south, **Platja d'Es Cavallet** and **Platja de Ses Salines**, are the most laid-back on the island and not for the easily shocked. Es Cavallet, over 1km long (⅔ mile), is designated a nudist beach and attracts a predominantly gay crowd. There are good facilities on the beach – shacks, bars, boutiques and watersports – but essentially little development and you can retreat to the sand dunes for peace and relative privacy.

Around the headland – a promontory of flat rocks on which the ancient watchtower **Torre de Ses Portes** keeps a lookout towards Formentera – is the island's other long beach. Ses Salines is 1.5km (1 mile) of soft sand backed by pine- and scrub-covered dunes which separate the open sea from the saltpans. The far end of Ses Salines, like the beach at Es Cavallet, is for nude sunbathing. Towards late morning, more and more boats arrive here from the marina at Eivissa and moor offshore while their passengers wade to the beach for a fresh fish lunch at one of the six or seven *chiringuitas*. Malibu is the *chiringuita* that attracts the most glamorous crowd.

Towards the end of the afternoon, people stroll up and down the beach in a kind of early *passeig*. From the road end, where the watersports equipment is kept, to the *torre*, the walk takes about half an hour – the rocks around the *torre* are unforgiving, so take a good pair of shoes

Bird Life

Huge flocks of migratory birds gather around Ses Salines in spring and autumn. The best time to arrive with a pair of binoculars is at dawn or dusk. Expect to see white wagtails, wild ducks, grey herons, storks, flamingos, egrets, the odd peregrine falcon, avocet and curlew. The birds stop here en route to and from North Africa, drawn by the plentiful food which is trapped in the saltpans.

The South at a Glance

Best Times to Visit

Being mainly off the beaten track, the scattered resorts of the south are quiet, becoming lively only in the tourist season of **May** to **October**. Even in the low season, however, local families flock to the beach restaurants for lunch on sunny weekends. The long expanses of beach at Es Cavallet and Ses Salines in the far southeast are a good place to escape the crowds in the summer months. Despite their beauty, they are rarely crowded. The advantage of staying in this area is that the sightseeing, shopping and nightlife of Eivissa are close by.

Local saints' days:
Sant Joan, 24 June;
Santa Maria, 5 August.

Getting There

Buses run from Eivissa and Sant Antoni to Sant Josép and Cala Vedella, but places like Es Cubells and the more remote *calas* are best reached by taxi. **Taxis** from the airport are reasonable; Sant Josép, for example, is only 14km (9 miles) away. Anyone staying in the Ses Salines area would also be best off taking a taxi from the airport – a couple of kilometres from the beaches.

Getting Around

The company with the best **bus services** locally is **Voramar El Gaucho**, tel: 971 32 03 82, connecting Sant Josép with Sant Antoni and Eivissa. **Boats** run from the busier *calas* to neighbouring bays and Eivissa is easily accessible for trips to Formentera. **Car** or **bicycle hire** is a good idea for anyone wanting to explore and there is some good walking country in this area. If you propose to do some serious **hiking**, invest in one of the Spanish military maps of the area as the walks are only erratically marked with red paint on stones and cairns. On the military maps, available from international map and travel bookshops overseas, the scale is 1:50,000 and all trails are marked.

Where to Stay

Luxury

Hotel Village Ibiza, Urbanización Calo d'en Real, Sant Josép, tel: 971 80 03 34, fax: 971 80 02 27. Pretty, Ibizenco-style hotel with 20 rooms, southwest of Sant Josép. Pool, tennis, golf-driving nets and a gymnasium.

Can Roca, Port des Torrent, Sant Josép, tel: 971 34 44 83, fax: 971 34 05 79. Luxurious, ochre-coloured villa in subtropical gardens with apartments, a studio and a house sleeping six. Pool, bar, sunny terrace and 50% discount at the golf course.

Hotel Les Jardins de Palerm, Sant Josép, tel: 971 80 03 18. Exquisite, 17th-century house furnished with antiques. Located in Sant Josép, surrounded by beautiful gardens.

Mid-range

Club Med Ibiza, Platja d'en Bossa, tel: 971 30 26 12. Large Club Med with seemingly endless facilities. Great for families – plenty of entertainment provided for children.

Club Cala Vedella, Apdo 17, 07830 Sant Josép, tel: 971 34 12 66, fax: 971 34 12 85. Big holiday club with extensive sporting facilities, set among pine trees on a hillside overlooking Cala Vedella. Tasteful, local-style architecture.

Hotel Tarida Beach, Platja de Cala Tarida, tel: 971 80 00 52. Huge, modern hotel on the beach with lots of facilities.

Club Cala Molí, Cala Molí, tel/fax: 971 80 60 02. Small hotel overlooking quiet cove.

Budget

Mary Sol, Playa de Ses Salines, tel: 971 39 65 84. *Hostal* right at the beach.

Escandell, Crtra Eivissa-Salines km 8.5, no tel or fax. Budget *hostal* near Salines.

Where to Eat

Restaurante Sa Tasca, Sant Agustí, tel: 971 34 37 03. International nouvelle cuisine in sophisticated but informal setting. Good wine list on offer.

The South at a Glance

Malibu, Platja de Ses Salines, tel: 971 39 65 80. Fresh fish and seafood in the most glamorous location of Ses Salines beach.

Blue Marlyn, Cal Jundal, Sant Josép, tel: 908 49 16 53. Fashionable café/bar.

C'As Mila, Cala Tarida, tel: 971 80 61 93. Sophisticated seafood restaurant on Cala Tarida beach. Open evenings and lunchtime.

Sa Soca, Crtra San Josép km2, tel: 971 34 16 20. Country restaurant outside Sant Antoni serving local game specialities.

KM5, On Ibiza-Sant Josep road at 5km mark. Fabulous Moroccan theme and lush gardens.

Ristorante Cala d'Hort. Busy beach restaurant, ideal for Sunday lunch. Paella, fish and sangría a speciality.

Tours and Excursions

There's plenty to see on this part of the island. Eivissa and Sant Antoni are both within easy reach by road. Boats hop from one *cala* to the next for a change of scene and there's some good, if strenuous, hiking around the cliffs.

Take time to visit the **salt-pans** at Ses Salines, preferably at sunrise or sunset, and **Cala d'Hort**, to admire the mysterious and jagged islet of **Es Vedrà**.

The **Hippodrome** at Sant Rafel is within easy reach, tel: 971 19 81 93, with trotting races on Tuesday and Saturday at 22:00 and 'chariot' races daily in summer.

Diving: three dive schools operate in this area:

Sea Horse Sub, Port des Torrent, tel/fax: 971 34 64 38; **Free Delfin Diving**, Hotel Club Delfin, Cala Codolar, tel: 971 80 62 10; **Orca Sub**, Club Hotel Tarida Beach, tel: 971 80 62 53. All three have English-speaking instructors.

Watersports equipment can be hired on the beaches of Cala Tarida, Ses Salines, Cala Codolar and Cala Vedella, with instruction available.

Shopping

The best shopping for **fashion** is in Eivissa, a short bus ride away, in the narrow streets around the Sa Marina district. For visitors interested in **ceramics**, explore the village of Sant Rafel on the Eivissa-Sant Antoni road. Huge *ceramicas* sell everything from ash trays and cookware to painted flower pots and statues for the garden. Most of the produce is very tasteful but if it says 'Made in Ibiza', don't be too sure. There is no clay on the island and many of the items are made on the mainland and exported to the Pitiusas for painting.

There are several markets within easy reach.

The weekly **hippie market** is at Es Canar on a Wednesday, accessible by bus or boat from Eivissa.

On Fridays, there's a **craft market** at Platja d'en Bossa in the Bahamas Hotel Complex and in Eivissa, every evening in the port.

Useful Contacts

The **tourist office** nearest to Sant Josép is in Sant Antoni, tel: 971 34 33 63, fax: 971 34 41 76. Visitors staying around Ses Salines should use the tourist office in Eivissa, tel: 971 30 19 00, fax: 971 33 29 59.

IBIZA - FORMENTERA
ETHYS
IB137

7
Formentera

The 'last paradise in the Mediterranean' as locals call it – the tiny island of Formentera – lies southeast of Ibiza, an hour away by ferry but in every other sense, a different world.

A long narrow strip of land, less than 1km (⅔ mile) wide in places, joins two remote rocky headlands, each capped by a lonely lighthouse. There is an overwhelming sense of peace and space on Formentera; from any point on the island there are sweeping views of grassy fields divided by low stone walls and long, untouched sandy beaches. The water is a luminous shade of turquoise and the few towns can hardly be described as such – more like a tiny cluster of white houses, baking in the hot sun.

This scene of rural serenity belies a violent and savage past. Always the poor relation of Ibiza, Formentera has never been any great centre of civilization. Megalithic man left stone structures, the Romans built roads and subsequent inhabitants erected a ring of stone watchtowers around the coast, but Formentera was always too plagued by **pirate attacks** for anyone to settle here comfortably. For several hundred years Formentera was uninhabited and used only as a base by **Barbary pirates** to attack Ibiza.

There are now some 5000 inhabitants, most of whom rely on tourism for a living. The island has plenty of modest accommodation – mainly in the little resort of **Es Pujols** – but most visitors come from Ibiza for the day, either on one of the many ferries that ply the shallow waters between the islands or on a luxury yacht, dropping in at the remote coves and beaches for a picnic lunch.

Don't Miss

*** **La Mola:** spectacular views from the island's remote headland. Don't miss the Jules Verne monument.
** **Migjorn:** extensive beaches.
** **Cap de Berberia:** a perfect place for walks.
* **Birdwatching:** visit the flocks at the island's saltpans.

Opposite: *Boats bob gently in the quiet harbour of La Savina at the north of Formentera.*

The North ★★

The port of **La Savina** is, for all visitors, their first impression of Formentera. Ferries dock here from Eivissa, Sant Antoni and Santa Eulària, as well as from Altea and Denia on the Spanish mainland. Sailing across from Ibiza is breathtaking, with fabulous views of the walls of Dalt Vila and the crumbling old houses of Sa Penya, the former fishing quarter, as the ship chugs out of the harbour.

The sea is shallow all the way across to Formentera, with uninhabited rocky islets and sandbanks strung together across the narrow straits. In centuries gone by, however, bad storms would mean that Formentera could be cut off from Ibiza for days at a time. The wink of lighthouses at night warns sailors off these hazard-strewn waters.

Most of the islands have names: **Negres**, **des Porc** and **Espardell**, which has a lighthouse. On **Espalmador** – an uninhabited rocky outcrop off Formentera's northernmost point – there's an 18th-century defence tower, **Sa Guardiola**, constructed in 1749. The tower is in a remarkable state of repair thanks to the restoration a few years ago, sponsored by the Conselleria de Cultura d'Eivissa i Formentera. Espalmador is fringed with exquisite beaches where the regional government has taken steps to protect the fragile environment by forbidding camping. Formentera's outlying islands are nonetheless popular with private yachts sailing over from Ibiza for the day.

On a calm day you can wade to Espalmador across the sand spits from the northernmost point, **Punta Trocadors**, at the end of a long spit of dazzling white sand backed by low-lying scrub-covered dunes accessible by dirt track.

Climate

Formentera enjoys much the same climate as Ibiza, although winds can whip across the narrow isthmus joining the two headlands, making cycling difficult work. The advantage for windsurfers, of course, is some of the best conditions in Europe. Formentera's beaches are almost always cooled by sea breezes, making the hot summers more tolerable but increasing the danger of sunburn.
In the low season, Formentera is cool and quiet and on a stormy day, the winds swirling around the lighthouse at La Mola, over foaming waves and moody skies, are certainly bracing.

La Savina ★

Providing a sheltered anchorage for yachts, **La Savina** has developed its infrastructure around the sailing community. Regattas are held here in July, during the celebrations of the **Virgen del Carmen**, the patron saint of sailors. Limestone, dried fish, fruit and sea salt all used to be exported from here to Ibiza but where the port was once filled with wooden frames for fish to be hung to dry in the sun, a semicircle of cafés and bars now lines the harbour. You will also find row after row of bicycles for hire – easily the best way to explore the island, which is only 20km (12½ miles) long. The roads have cycle lanes and the rental bikes are in good condition. Alternatively, there are mopeds and cars.

Saltpans ★

Like Ibiza, Formentera has saltpans which, together with the natural saltwater lagoon of **Estany Pudent** and its smaller neighbour, **Estany des Peix**, form an area of natural wetland. The saltpans are half-heartedly tended by Formentera's older generation but it is unlikely that their successors will carry on the tradition. Instead, this remote area has become a sanctuary for thousands of migratory birds. Flamingos are rare nowadays, but seagulls, herons, plovers and egrets flock here. Skeletal windmills around the saltpans, formerly used to pump in water from the sea, add atmosphere.

Lizards

The species of lizard native to the Pitiusas, *Podarsis pityusensis*, has more than 40 subspecies, each of which has adapted to a different habitat on the islands. On the sand spits of Formentera the lizards are almost white, while those on Es Vedrà are bright green. On the islet of Murada they have a blueish tinge, and elsewhere, the reptiles are almost black.
Known locally as *sargantanes*, the lizards, which are quite tame, were almost endangered because of a flourishing pet trade. Now they are protected by law.

Below: *Like Ibiza, Formentera has its own saltpans, though they are barely worked today.*

Typical Formentera

Despite its proximity to Ibiza, Formentera has several unique features.
Shopping: look out for traditional Formenteran knitwear, soft and cream-coloured.
Megalithic sites: Ca Na Costa is the most exciting archaeological find in the Pitiusas, dating from prehistoric times.
Wine: try some of Formentera's strong red wine, sold in very small, out-of-the-way bars and cafés.
Food: try island honey and the local sheep and goat's milk cheeses.
Espalmador: wade over to this tiny, uninhabited island and take an invigorating mudbath in the lagoon there. The place has never been developed as a spa but the mud is supposed to cure aches and pains.

Ca Na Costa ★

A turn-off from the road from La Savina to the resort of Es Pujols leads to **Ca Na Costa**, the most important archaeological find on either of the islands. Megalithic remains, identified as a tomb dating from 2000BC, were discovered here in 1978. The site is covered and protected by a fence so you can view the structure from all angles. Composed of seven large, upright slabs of limestone, the burial chamber is surrounded by two rings of buttress stones. Radial slabs encircle the exterior. Archaeologists consider Ca Na Costa a shining example of architecture remarkably sophisticated for its time. If it looks like a pile of stones, visit the **Museu Arqueològic** in Eivissa, where finds from the site help explain pre-Bronze Age life.

Es Pujols ★

The main – and only substantial – resort on Formentera is **Es Pujols**, east of Estany Pudent and an easy cycle ride from the port. Bars and restaurants are concentrated here and the little town is relatively lively in summer. A must for anyone on the hippie trail is **Fonda Pepe** at nearby Sant Ferran. Once the meeting place for hippies on the island, the old bar is actually a bus station now.

East of Es Pujols, there's an 18th-century watchtower on the headland. The latter is protected by law, thus preventing the resort from spreading out of control.

Below: *Deep-blue sea fringes the beach at Es Pujols.*

THROWING FOR A CHICKEN

An old tradition known as *tirar a es gall* is alive and well in Formentera, a game for which the prize is a plump chicken. Thirteen pins are arranged on a field or country lane and the players each throw two balls made of heavy juniper wood. The balls are bowled with some force and spectators are careful to keep out of the way. Each player throws the balls four times and the one who knocks down the most pins wins the chicken.

SANT FRANCESC XAVIER ★★

The main road from the port leads uphill to **Sant Francesc**, Formentera's capital, passing the only petrol station, which closes at night. Sant Francesc is really little more than a straggly, sleepy village clustered around the crossroads that leads in one direction to Sant Ferran and in the other down to Cap de Berberia. There are a few bars and cafés around the square as well as shops where, in spring and summer, you can stock up on sheep's or goat's cheese from the island – ideal for a picnic lunch. As a point of interest, the workshop **Can Vicenc des Ferrer** in Sant Francesc makes traditional musical instruments from products grown on the island. And don't miss shops selling the local knitwear – cream-coloured and extremely soft.

Above: *Mainland pottery for sale in Sant Francesc.*
Below: *Sant Francesc's church was used as a shelter during 18th-century pirate attacks.*

Also on the square is the solid, fortress-like **church** which has defended the hilltop against pirates since the 18th century. The church is built in the very traditional Ibizenco style, with few adornments. It was constructed in 1726 at the request of the parishioners of the

island. The building also doubled up as a fortified refuge from the many pirate attacks, although it was only used for this purpose for a few years until the Barbary raids ceased in 1738.

Accurate records of the church and its community have been kept over the last 250 years; the record for 1784, for example, states that the high altar was plated with gold and adorned with a statue of San Francisco Javier. The priest's living quarters are located above the nave and on the patio there's a cistern; as Formentera has no water supplies, everybody always has to collect any available rainwater.

Also worth looking for in Sant Francesc is the tiny chapel, **Sa Tanca Vella**, which dates back to the 14th century. The archbishop of the time, Pere du Clasquerí, authorized the construction of a chapel for the first wave of settlers from Ibiza, who felt far removed from their home parish of Santa Maria (now Eivissa). The chapel was built in a simple, rectangular design with a barrel-vaulted roof, close to the cave of Sant Velero to whom it is dedicated.

For many years, the chapel was incorporated into a farmhouse of the same name. However, the farmhouse was demolished in 1985 in order to reveal the monument as a stand-alone feature.

Herbal Pleasures

Native plants have long been used as cures on Ibiza and Formentera. White henbane and opium poppy have both been used as painkillers in the past and at one point – enjoyed by hippies and locals alike – cannabis was grown casually in the *torrents*, the seasonal rivers. Alongside this, *tobac pota*, a special, local kind of tobacco with a strong smell, has been grown for a long time. When the cultivation of this plant was banned in a Royal Order, there was such a fuss that the law had to be revoked. The plant may now be grown on Ibiza and Formentera but not exported.

Flower Watch

Something is always in bloom on the islands – just venture outside the resort and soak up the scenery.

January: yellow mimosa
February: pink and white almond blossom all over the island
March–June: white daisies, followed by whole fields of poppies, cornflowers, cow parsley and the yellow flowers of the prickly pear; wild thyme scents the air
July–August: gardens are brilliant with purple bougainvillea and scented with pink honeysuckle
September: scarlet geraniums, pink and purple petunias and dahlias
October: prickly pears bear their large, yellow fruits
December–January: fruit appears on the citrus trees.

Cap de Berberia

South of Sant Francesc is the wild, pine-clad Cap de Berberia, its arid soil softened by the pink flowers of wild thyme in May and June. The pine trees once grew more densely; apparently the American Depression of 1929 is to blame for the bleakness of the area today. Many people had emigrated to the New World from Formentera but were forced to return when bad times struck America. The only work they could find on Formentera was as charcoal burners, and the only wood to burn was pine, which never really recovered from the decimation.

Cap de Berberia is one of the earliest settlements in the Pitiusas, with evidence of a large population in the first half of the second millenium BC, the Neolithic and Bronze ages. The excavations, signposted 'Cap de Berberia II', are situated off the main road leading from Sant Francesc to the headland. The site is actually fenced in but quite a lot can be seen from the protective grille. Limestone slabs form the outline of primitive dwellings, grouped around a central open area. The site was occupied for some time, and extra walls were added over the centuries.

A beach on the west of this cape, **Cala Saona**, is popular with locals at the weekend and its coarse white sand and pine-covered, rust-coloured cliffs attract a smattering of visitors in summer. To experience the real bleakness of Formentera, however, walk between the two 18th-century watchtowers, **Torre de la Gavina** on the west side and **Torre des Garroveret** in the far south. With little but seabirds and insects for company, the coast path winds along rugged cliffs lined with wind-stunted trees to the solitary lighthouse on the point, from which, people say, you can see Africa on a clear day. There's a cave in the cliff face, **Cova Foradada**.

Opposite: *Sa Tanca Vella, with its distinctive barrel-vaulted roof.*

Below: *Wild and largely untouched, Cap de Berberia is covered in pines.*

Walking on Formentera

Sunglasses, sunblock and good walking shoes are essential – even in spring the sun is strong, and many of the paths involve picking your way over low stone walls and through thistles. Formenteran people are relaxed and friendly, but do show respect in the villages and dress modestly. Don't walk through a village in swimwear and do cover your shoulders to enter a church. Incidentally, the strange-smelling tobacco smoked in remote areas is *pota* (not cannabis, as the name might imply), grown in secluded patches and surprisingly smooth should someone offer you a puff. Walking means you'll stumble across some off-the-beaten-track places, ideal for trying the country wine (*vino de pagés*), a distinctive dry red.

Central Formentera ★★★

Formentera's two capes are joined by a narrow isthmus, scattered with whitewashed farmhouses, patches of arable land and small pine woods. One main road runs the length of the island but a better alternative for cyclists is the **Camino Viejo** which runs parallel to it.

Camino Viejo ★★

At the entrance to Sant Francesc, head towards Cap de Berberia and veer off to the left after about 100m (330ft). A small sign says 'Camino Viejo'. This old mule track is tarred in places and is far more peaceful than the main road which, despite having separate cycle lanes, can be stressful in fast-moving traffic.

The **Camino Viejo** was once the main road across the island, used by monks leading mules laden with wine from the plateau of **La Mola** to the port of **La Savina**. At times, the tarmac becomes a dirt track, so a mountain bike is essential. The *camino* does run the entire length of the island but becomes very difficult to follow and you'll have to pick your way across stony farm tracks. However, getting lost is not easy as the headland of La Mola is always visible and on the left, you can see the shoreline.

Using this old road, cyclists will come across some fascinating features of old Formentera. Look out for circles of stones in the fields – these are the remains of charcoal burners which generated the heat for producing the lime used for whitewashing houses. Wells are usually surrounded by brickwork and if you see a tiny door built into the outside wall of a house, it's a cool larder, dating back to the days before refrigerators. Also look out for giant fig trees, their canopies supported by smaller trees, and hoopoe birds, common on Formentera. The hoopoe is reddish-pink with black-and-white wings and tail feathers.

Below: *From La Mola the whole central isthmus of the island is visible.*

Above: *Formentera is a cycling paradise with country tracks and low stone walls.*

Other than farmland, there is little development along this stretch of the island. The southern side, behind a barrier of pine woods, consists of one long stretch of beach known as **Platja de Migjorn**. At the far end there's a big holiday village called **Maryland**, but before reaching the turn-off there are plenty of trails over the dunes to deserted spots.

The north side of the isthmus is rockier, ending at the tiny cluster of bungalows and holiday apartments known as **Es Caló**. Here, the water is an astonishing shade of turquoise and the only signs of activity are a few fishing nets and boats pulled up on the shore.

Confusingly, there's another Es Caló, **Es Caló de Mort**, on the south side of the road. This miniature harbour of crystal clear water protects a semicircle of wooden runners for launching fishing boats. The cove was used in Roman times and at nearby **Can Blai** is the remainder of a Roman camp, located at the km10 marker on the road to La Mola. The square-shaped site contains five rectangular structures which would probably have formed towers made of blocks of limestone and filled with lime cement. The site was excavated in the 1970s but the very sparse nature of the remains, with no mosaics or hints about the lifestyle of their inhabitants, suggests that this was probably a small *castellum*, or defensive fortress, lived in only some of the time.

Best Beaches for Baring All

Ibiza and Formentera have several beaches where naturism is permitted:

Platja de Migjorn: long stretch of sand with undeveloped parts that are protected by dunes

Platja de Ses Salines: nude bathing at the end closest to the watchtower

Platja d'Es Cavallet: almost entirely nude beach, popular with gays

S'Aigua Blanca: tiny, pebbly beach in northeast of Ibiza at the base of steep cliffs; very quiet

LA MOLA ★★★

The promontory at Formentera's far end is completely flat on top, ending abruptly in steep cliffs falling into a choppy sea. There is a **lighthouse** as well as the inevitable **defence tower**. For cyclists, the upward climb to La Mola is the only real challenge on the island, with the road following hairpins through pine woods. The view from the top is rewarding as the whole island lies stretched out below, the narrow isthmus visibly vulnerable to the open seas. There is one theory that the name Formentera comes from the Latin *promontorium* meaning promontory, not 'forment', the word used by the Romans for wheat.

With just one village and a few scattered farms, being on La Mola gives a real sensation of open space. The hamlet of **El Pilar** has a diminutive, Ibizenco-style church, **Nostra Senyora del Pilar**, built towards the end of

FIGS

The common fig tree, identified by its big, acid-green leaves, is cultivated all over the Mediterranean and was particularly popular in Roman times for its sweet, exotic-looking fruit. Believed by the Romans to have aphrodisiac properties, figs are highly nutritious and even today have many uses: they are eaten fresh; dried whole or compressed; or seasoned with wild thyme to make *frígola*. The skins of the fruit make a nourishing meal for pigs. Figs are also associated with longevity; giant trees on Formentera are said to explain the long life of the residents there.

the 18th century. There are a couple of shops worth visiting: a pottery at **Can Gabrielet** and a wool shop opposite the bar in El Pilar, where you can buy knitwear typical of Formentera. Otherwise, the top of La Mola consists of little more than golden wheatfields, stubby vines and shady carob groves. One monument worth exploring, however, is the **old windmill**, located a couple of hundred metres south of the road leading up to the lighthouse. Built in 1778, the windmill has recently been acquired by the Fundació Islas Balears, a cultural conservation movement. It still works, grinding corn as it has done for over 200 years.

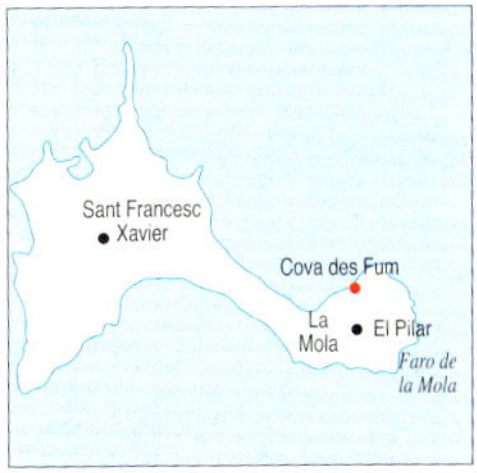

PARDELA HUNTING

Until fairly recently, Formenterans engaged in the dangerous practice of dangling from the steep cliffs at La Mola to catch the pardela, a seabird. The bird was known locally as *virot* and the activity, *virotar*, became an official verb in the Catalan language. Now the bird is protected and no longer eaten, and the word has all but disappeared from the Catalan language.

Faro de la Mola **

Formentera's lonely lighthouse, **Faro de la Mola**, has kept sailors off the treacherous rocks since 1861, its beam reaching 60km (37½ miles) out to sea. An unlikely visitor was the author **Jules Verne** who, taken with the wild solitude of the place, used it as a setting for his 1877 novel *Journey Round the Solar System*. A monument to Monsieur Verne stands by the lighthouse. Should you be on Formentera on New Year's Eve, a local tradition is to see in the New Year at the bar **Es Puig** and then to settle by the lighthouse throughout the chilly night to greet the first sunrise.

Just off the road here is the **Cova des Fum**, a cave with a grisly past. According to legend, invading Normans in 1108 tortured and burned Arab inhabitants in this cave.

Opposite top: *Faro de la Mola is the site of a traditional New Year's celebration.*

Opposite bottom: *The old windmill near El Pilar still continues to grind corn today.*

Left: *Contemplating the edge at La Mola: next stop Menorca!*

Formentera at a Glance

Best Times to Visit

In **winter**, Formentera is very, very quiet and almost all hotels, guesthouses and restaurants close, as do bicycle hire shops.
Spring is a beautiful time to visit, when carpets of wildflowers cover the island and the heady scent of wild thyme and rosemary fills the air. Temperatures are generally mild and cycling is pleasant.
In **summer**, although the island is cooled by sea breezes, cycling is hot work and visitors will be less inclined to make long forays into the countryside. All facilities, however, are open, the little towns pleasantly lively and conditions for sunbathing and windsurfing ideal. Certainly, in July and August, Formentera is a breath of fresh air after the crowded beaches of Ibiza.
Autumn, particularly **September**, is the best time for scuba diving in the clear waters off Formentera as the Mediterranean has had all summer to warm up.

Local saints' days:
Sant Ferran, 30 May;
Virgen del Carmen, 16 July;
Sant Jaume, 25 July;
Sant Maria, 5 August;
Sant Francesc, 3 December;
Nuestra Señora del Pilar, 12 December.

Getting There

Formentera has no airport, which is part of its charm. The only access is by **boat** and several **ferry lines** operate between Ibiza and the mainland. Look carefully at the schedule before booking a return ticket; some lines, for example, have convenient crossings from Eivissa in the morning but a three-hour gap between departures in the evening. Sometimes it's better to take the Flebasa **hydrofoil** there and a ferry back. Tickets are bought direct from the various ferry company offices on the dock in either Eivissa or La Savina, or from travel agents. Timetables are published in the newspaper and are also available from the tourist office.
Ferry companies:
Pitra, tel: 971 19 10 68. Car ferry from Denia to Formentera.
Flebasa, tel: 971 31 30 05. Services from Eivissa by hydrofoil, taking 30 minutes.
Trasmapi, tel: 971 31 40 05. Car ferry from Eivissa, 1 hour.
Trasmediterranea, tel: 971 31 50 50. Car ferry from Eivissa and services from mainland.

Getting Around

The most environmentally friendly way to visit Formentera is by **bicycle**. Rental shops line the quayside in La Savina and prices are reasonable. Hire a mountain bike if you plan to venture offroad, as trails are rough. Stamina is required to make it from one end of the island to the other and back in a day – a round trip of some 42km (25 miles). Alternatively, hire a **moped** or **motorbike**, a good way to see more of the island on a daytrip. There are also several **car rental** companies for visitors with small children or a lot of baggage. **Taxis** run from the port and from Sant Francesc and Es Pujols. **Buses**, however, are somewhat unreliable.
Taxis: Sant Francesc, tel: 971 32 30 16; La Savina, tel: 971 32 20 02; Es Pujols, tel: 971 32 80 16.
Car hire: Avis, tel: 971 32 21 23. **Autos Formentera**, tel: 971 32 21 56. **Hertz**, tel: 971 32 22 42.

Where to Stay

Accommodation is far more modest than on Ibiza and most establishments are either apartments or simple *hostals*. There are two holiday villages, Club La Mola and Maryland.
Formentera Reservations, useful on-line reservations agency for hotels and apartments, tel: 971 32 32 41, fax: 971 32 30 96, website: www.formenterareservations.com
The **Formentera Hotel Association**, tel: 971 32 20 57, fax: 971 32 28 25, provides a useful brochure listing accommodation, with pictures of each property.

Formentera at a Glance

LUXURY

Hotel Club La Mola, Platja de Migjorn, tel: 971 32 80 69, fax: 971 32 80 69. Large, low-rise holiday complex on the island's longest beach. Plenty of facilities.

Club Maryland, Platja de Migjorn, tel: 971 32 80 34, fax: 971 32 82 45. Individual villas and apartments set in the pine trees at eastern end of Migjorn beach.

Hotel Formentera Playa, Platja de Migjorn, tel: 971 32 80 00, fax: 971 32 80 35. Large, 315-room, 3-star hotel with extensive facilities.

MID-RANGE

Club Punta Prima, Es Pujols, tel: 971 32 82 44, fax: 971 32 81 28. Attractive, low-rise building situated on lovely beachfront near Es Pujols.

Hostal Residencia Sa Volta, Calle Miramar 94, Es Pujols, tel: 971 32 81 25, fax: 971 32 82 28. Small *hostal* with bar situated in the town centre.

Hostal Voramar, Avda Miramar, Es Pujols, tel: 971 32 81 19, fax: 971 32 81 19. Pleasant *hostal* in the centre of Es Pujols with bar, terrace and games room.

Hostal Cala Saona, Cala Saona, tel: 971 32 20 30, fax: 971 32 25 09. Two-star hotel with large pool, located on beautiful beach on the west side of Cap de Berberia.

BUDGET

Hostal La Savina, Avda Mediterrania 22–40, La Savina, tel: 971 32 22 79, fax: 971 32 22 79. 40-room *hostal* with pretty terrace overlooking the port.

Hostal Levante, Calle Espalmador 21–31, Es Pujols, tel: 971 32 81 93, fax: 971 32 86 41. *Hostal* with restaurant and bar close to centre of Es Pujols.

Hostal Maysi, Platja de Migjorn, tel: 971 32 85 47. *Hostal* with 25 rooms, terrace and pool, directly on the beach.

Fonda Can Rafalet, Apartado 225, Es Caló, tel: 908 13 65 92. Tiny restaurant with rooms on the beach.

WHERE TO EAT

Es Mirador, La Mola km14.3, tel: 971 32 70 37. Fresh fish and paella. Stunning views over the island from the terrace.

Es Puig, Punta de la Mola. Basic food in remote setting, next to the lighthouse.

Can Rafalet, Es Caló, tel: 971 32 70 16. Paella and fish in scenic beachfront location.

La Formenterena, Platja de Migjorn km 8.7, tel: 971 32 87 53. Local dishes on the beach, accompanied by flamenco and guitar music.

Sa Gavina, Platja d'es Pujols, tel: 971 32 83 51. Award-winning fish and rice dishes on the beach in Es Pujols.

Bellavista, Passeig de la Marina 8, Ses Savines, tel: 971 32 22 36, fax: 971 32 22 36. Ibizenco and international cuisine in the port.

Blue Bar, Platja de Migjorn. Lively bar on the beach.

SHOPPING

Good buys unique to Formentera include the local *hierbas* liqueur, cheese, honey, Formentera pottery, and knitwear.

TOURS AND EXCURSIONS

Guided tours bookable on the island are very limited and the majority of visitors travel around independently.

Some taxi drivers offer guided tours, tel: 971 32 20 16 or 971 32 80 16.

Travel agent: Viajes Urbis, Passeig de la Marina s/n, Ses Savines, tel: 971 32 22 99.

The tourist board produces a leaflet, *Circuitos Verdes*, of recommended walking and cycling routes on the island. Most of the tracks are very short but provide attractive alternatives to walking along the road.

USEFUL CONTACTS

Formentera Mar La Savina, tel: 971 32 32 35.Complex in the marina with watersports and equipment rental.

Sailing school (Escuela de vela Es Pujols), On the beach at Es Pujols.

Tourist Board La Savina, tel: 971 32 20 57.

Travel Tips

Tourist Information

The Spanish Tourist Board has offices in the United Kingdom (London); the USA (Chicago, Los Angeles, Miami and New York); Canada (Toronto); Australia (Sydney); and most European countries. Ibiza has its own tourist board with several offices located around the island. **Head office:** Consell Insular de Ibiza i Formentera, tel: 971 39 73 00.
Local branches: Eivissa, Av. Anderes, tel: 971 30 19 00, fax: 971 30 16 62; Santa Eulària, Mariano Riquer Wallis s/n, tel: 971 33 07 28, fax: 971 33 29 59; Sant Antoni, Passeig de ses Fonts s/n, tel: 971 34 33 63, fax: 971 34 41 76.
Hotel Association: Historiador José Clapés 4, Eivissa, tel: 971 30 46 43, www.ibiza–hotels.com
Airport information: tel: 971 30 12 54, websites: www.ibiza-spotlight.com www.ibiza-online.com www.caib.es (Balearic government site)

Entry Requirements

All visitors need a passport or, in certain cases, an identity card. Citizens of Andorra, Lichtenstein, Monaco, Switzerland, and countries within the EC need only present an identity card, with the exception of Denmark and the UK, citizens of which need a passport. UK visitors must have a full 10-year passport. US, Canadian and Japanese citizens require a passport but no visa. Visas are required for citizens of Australia and New Zealand. All visitors can stay up to 90 days, after which time a residence permit is required.

Customs

The maximum allowance for duty-free items brought into Spain from outside the EU is as follows: one litre of spirits or two of fortified wine; two litres of wine and 200 cigarettes. Duty-free was abolished within the EU in 1999. If bought and duties paid in the EU, the amounts are 10 litres of spirits, 90 litres of wine and 110 litres of beer, for private consumption only. However, there is little point bringing wine or beer into Spain, as they are cheap locally. Spanish and foreign currency, bank drafts and traveller's cheques can be imported and exported without being declared up to a limit of 1,000,000 pesetas.

Health Requirements

No vaccinations are required to enter Spain and the only real health hazards are the occasional upset stomach and the sun, which is very strong during the summer months of June to September.
EU citizens qualify for free medical treatment on presentation of the appropriate form. Visitors from elsewhere should arrange their own travel and medical insurance.

Getting There

By air: The airport is 7.5km (4½ miles) from Eivissa, in the southeast of the island. Most flights in the tourist season are charters from the UK, Germany and other north European destinations, with several an hour in peak season. Scheduled services operate from Ibiza to the Spanish mainland, the other islands of the Balearics and international destinations. Iberia Airlines: Avda Espanya 34, Eivissa, tel: 971 30 09 54.

By sea: Car and passenger ferries operate from Formentera, Palma de Mallorca, Denia and Valencia. Ibiza–Formentera: **Transmapi**, tel: 971 30 01 00, and **Feblasa**, tel: 971 34 28 71. Ibiza–Barcelona, Valencia and Palma: **Trasmediterranea SA**, tel: 971 31 50 50. Sant Antoni–Denia: **Feblasa**, tel: 971 34 28 71.

By road: Travellers bringing their own car from the mainland and residing outside the EC must have a Green Card, as third party insurance is compulsory. An international driving licence is also required. Driving in Spain is on the right-hand side. For visitors driving to the ports on the mainland, en route to Ibiza, road conditions and travel information are available in Spanish on the Teleruta service, tel: 91 535-2222.

What to Pack

Nightlife

If you plan to take advantage of Ibiza's famous nightlife, high fashion is essential! This is a cosmopolitan island and to keep up with the 'beautiful people', you'll need plenty of outfits, the more outrageous the better. Some people wait until they arrive to buy a wardrobe. Otherwise, evenings are very casual; in the beach resorts you can go to dinner in shorts, although everybody dresses up in Eivissa and Sant Antoni.
Ibiza's own fashion label is called Ad Lib, available in shops all around the port.

Hiking

Remember to bring sunglasses and a hat for the summer and good walking boots if you propose to go hiking.

Sightseeing

Casual wear is fine for sightseeing. Show respect when entering the cathedral or churches – ladies should wear longish skirts and cover their shoulders, and men should not wear shorts. In the low season, take something warmer for the evenings, which can get chilly.

Money Matters

The peseta has been replaced by the Euro, which is divided into 100 cents. Notes come in denominations of 5, 10, 20, 50, 100, 200 and 500 Euros and coins in 1, 2, 5, 10, 20 and 50 cents and 1 and 2 Euros. All major credit cards are accepted although some country restaurants and small tapas bars may require cash. Banking hours are 09.00–14.00 Mon-Fri and 09.00–13.00 on Saturday, although they vary occasionally. Holders of cards bearing the Visa, MasterCard, Cirrus and Plus signs can use Spanish automatic tellers, which have instructions in English. However, take note that a fee is always charged for this. Traveller's cheques and cash can be changed in banks as well as the bureaux de change which operate in all the main resorts, and at larger hotels. Sales tax (IVA) is currently 16% and is not always included in the price, so beware.

USEFUL EIVISSENC PHRASES

Si, No, Val • Yes, No, Okay
Si us plau, Gràcies (**Merci** in north Catalunya and Ibiza) • Please, Thank you
Hola, Adéu • Hello, Goodbye
Bona tarde/nit • Good afternoon/night
Com va? • How are you?
(No) ho entenc • I (don't) understand
Parleu anglés? • Do you speak English?
Em dic... • My name is...
Es massa car • It's too expensive
On és...? • Where is...?
Qué hi ha per menjar? • What is there to eat?

Tipping is optional; around 10% of the price of a meal is acceptable. Petrol pump attendants and taxi drivers also invariably appreciate a small tip.

Accommodation

Hotels are rated according to a star system with five stars being the highest. 'Gran Luxe' signifies a particularly luxurious hotel. Apartment hotels follow the same grades, the only difference being that they have cooking facilities in the rooms. *Hostals* and *pensions*, more basic establishments, are graded from one to three stars. Campsites are rated luxury, first, second and third class. There are seven in total on Ibiza. Each region, however, is responsible for its own classification, so accommodation gradings will vary. Most hotels belong to the Hotel Federation, tel: 971 30 46 43.

Eating Out

Tapas bars, *tascas*, *bodegas*, *cervecerías* and *tabernas* are all types of bars serving food. A *comedor* is a simple dining room, usually attached to a bar while a *venta* is a similar set-up in the countryside, usually with a small shop as well. A *marisquería* specializes in seafood and an *asado* in barbecued food.

Transport

Good, **tarred roads** connect Eivissa, Sant Antoni, Santa Eulària, Sant Josép, Sant Miquel and Portinatx. Secondary roads are well signposted. What looks like a minor road on a map, for example a road leading down to a beach, may well be a rutted dirt track.

Petrol stations are widely available with leaded and lead-free petrol and diesel. Some are self-service and some have attendants. Formentera has only one petrol station, which closes at night.

There are **car rental** companies in Eivissa, Sant Antoni, Santa Eulària and Es Canar, as well as at several smaller resorts and at the airport. Many also rent motorbikes and bicycles. Formentera has several rental companies based around La Savina.

Hertz
tel: 971 80 91 78.
Autos Isla Blanca (head office in Eivissa), tel: 971 30 44 31.
Avis (head office in Eivissa), tel: 971 80 91 17.

To hire a car, drivers must be over 21 with at least one year's experience. Never leave anything in a car as vehicle crime is a problem.

On the mainland, speed limits are 120kph (75mph) on *autopistas*; 120kph (75mph), 100kph (65mph) or 80kph (50mph) according to signs on *autovias* (dual carriageways); 90kph (55mph) on country roads; and 60kph (40mph) on urban roads. Only the latter two apply to Ibiza, which has no dual carriageways. Stiff, on-the-spot speeding fines are not uncommon. The wearing of seatbelts is compulsory in the front and, if fitted, in the back. Motorcyclists must wear safety helmets by law.

Buses operate to all the main towns and villages on the island. Timetables are available from the local tourist board or are posted up at the bus station. The buses are cheap, efficient and prompt. Four companies split the island up roughly between them: **Autocares Sant Antoni**, tel: 971 19 2456; **Lucas Costa**, tel: 971 31 49 00; **Voramar**, tel: 971 34 03 82; **H.F. Vilàs**, tel: 971 31 16 01.

Buses usually stop runnning at about 23:00 but Autocares Sant Antoni operates the 'disco bus' between Sant Antoni, Sant Rafel and Eivissa hourly from midnight to 06:00.

Ibiza's taxis are convenient and not particularly expensive. They can be hailed on the street or found at taxi ranks. A green light on the top means the taxi is free. Drivers do not tend to speak English and while all taxis are metered, there is a fixed price for certain routes, so establish an understanding before setting off. There's an extra tax for travel with large pieces of luggage. Tips are appreciated but not expected.

Conversion Chart

From	To	Multiply By
Millimetres	Inches	0.0394
Metres	Yards	1.0936
Metres	Feet	3.281
Kilometres	Miles	0.6214
Square kilometres	Square miles	0.386
Hectares	Acres	2.471
Litres	Pints	1.760
Kilograms	Pounds	2.205
Tonnes	Tons	0.984

Business Hours

Shops and businesses generally open from 09:00 or 10:00 to 13:30 or 14:00, close for a siesta and then reopen from 16:00 to 20:00. Some businesses start much earlier, around 08:00 and work straight through to 15:00 with no siesta. Hours also change in the summer. Most supermarkets close for lunch. Shops in Eivissa's Sa Marina district stay open until around midnight in summer.

Lunch tends to be served from about 13:00 to 16:00, with dinner from 20:00 (sometimes earlier for the benefit of tourists) to 23:00. Bars and clubs stay open late – sometimes until 05:00. One club, Space, opens at 06:00 and closes at midday.

Time

Spain is on GMT+1 hour in winter and on GMT+2 hours from the last Sunday in March to the last Sunday in October.

Communications

The international dialling code for Spain is +34. Each province has its own dialling prefix. The code for Ibiza (and the other Balearic islands) is 971 when dialling from overseas and 971 when dialling from within Spain.
Full instructions on the use of public telephones are shown in English in the kiosk. Rates are cheaper between 22:00 and 08:00. Public telephones take coins of 5, 25 and 100 pesetas. To call overseas, dial 07 and wait for the tone to change before dialling the country code and the number. Telephone cards can be bought from Telefonica offices or tobacconists.
The main post office is at Carrer Madrid s/n, Eivissa, tel: 971 31 13 80. Sant Antoni and Santa Eulària also have post offices. Formentera's post office is at Plaça de la Constitució, Sant Francesc, tel: 971 32 02 43. Stamps can be purchased from tobacconists and hotel receptions.

Media

Spanish and international newspapers are widely available. Ibiza does, however, have two papers of its own, *Diaria de Ibiza*, tel: 971 30 16 04, and *La Prensa de Ibiza*, tel: 971 31 68 11. There are three local radio stations, Radio Popular (81.9FM), Radio Ibiza Ser (98.1FM) and Radio Diario de Ibiza (102.8FM). The two national TV channels are TVE1 and TVE2. Spain also receives a number of cable and satellite channels.

Electricity

The power system is 220 or 225 volts AC. Older buildings occasionally have 110 or 125 volts AC and should be treated with extreme caution. Two-pin plugs are used. If bringing electrical equipment, Americans will need a transformer, British visitors an adaptor.

Weights and Measures

Spain uses the metric system.

Health Precautions

Tap water is safe but extremely unpleasant in Ibiza, both for drinking and washing in. Invest in several bottles of mineral water, available everywhere, with or without gas.
An excess of sun and sangría are the worst health problems encountered by most people! Use a high factor sun protection cream, wear a hat and take special care during the height of summer. Be sure to drink bottled water if you get a stomach upset. A mosquito repellent is also a good idea.

Castilian Road Signs

Ceda el paso • Give way
Circunvalación or **ronda** • Ring road or bypass
Cruce peligroso • Dangerous crossroads
Despacio • Slow
Desviación • Diversion
Entrada • Entrance
Estacionamento prohibido • No parking
Obras • Workmen
Prohibido adelantar • No overtaking
Puesto de soccoro • First aid post
Sin plomo • Unleaded petrol
Salida • Exit
Salida de camiones • Lorry exit

Health Services

Spanish pharmacists are highly trained and can dispense medicines often only available on prescription elsewhere. Opening hours are 09:00 to 13:30 and 17:00 to 20:30 (with the occasional half-hour variation). Every area of Ibiza has a duty pharmacy with a 24-hour service, the address of which is displayed on the doors of other pharmacies. Formentera has a pharmacy in Sant Francesc and one in Es Pujols.

Security

Petty crime is the only likely problem travellers will encounter, although the Dalt Vila has its no-go areas at night, populated by drug addicts. Follow normal precautions: don't leave anything in a car; be careful with purses and wallets; don't wear

Eivissenc for Reading Maps

Ajuntament • Town Hall
Avinguda • Avenue
Barri • Suburb or quarter
Carrer • Street
Casa • House
Passeig • Promenade or boulevard (also the evening stroll thereon)
Plaça • Square
Platja • Beach
Portal • Gateway
Seu • Cathedral
Serra • Mountain range

ostentatious jewellery and use hotel safe deposit boxes. Sexual harassment is not generally a problem and as the streets are always so busy at night, women should feel safe walking around the resorts.

Emergencies

There are three different numbers for three separate police services. **Policia Municipal** (the urban police) are found in Eivissa, tel: 971 31 58 61; Sant Antoni, tel: 971 340 502; Santa Eulària, tel: 971 33 08 41; and Sant Joan, tel: 971 33 30 05. **Guardia Civil** (rural and traffic police) are found in Eivissa, tel: 092; Sant Antoni, tel: 092; Santa Eulària, tel: 092. **Policia Nacional** (which deals with more serious crimes), is in Eivissa, tel: 091. Hospital Can Misses, tel: 39 70 00. **Ambulance** and **Fire Brigade**, tel: 112

Etiquette

Topless sunbathing is acceptable on the beaches and nude sunbathing on S'Aigua Blanca, Ses Salines and Es Cavallet. More modesty is appropriate inland, particularly in villages. Visitors are advised to adopt the Spanish siesta routine; visiting sights and expecting to have meetings during the early afternoon is not appropriate. Expect to have dinner late; most Spaniards eat at 22:00 or 23:00 in summer, earlier in winter. Don't even contemplate turning up at a club until after midnight – you'll be the only one there.

Language

Catalan (the local dialect is Eivissenc) is undergoing a strong revival in the Balearics, Catalunya, parts of Aragón, Valencia, Andorra, parts of the French Pyrenees and even areas of Italy. Catalan itself is a language, not a dialect, and is spoken by some 10 million people – more widespread, in other words, than Danish or Norwegian. In Catalunya, particularly Barcelona, Catalan is the main business language today.
In remote villages of Ibiza and Formentera, Eivissenc has always been spoken, despite being banned under General Franco. But because the language was not taught for many years, many older people cannot read or write it. While Castilian Spanish continues to be taught alongside Catalan in schools, road signs, some newspapers and conversation are now generally in Catalan and more and more place names and signposting are being converted. Using an up-to-date map is a good idea for getting around Ibiza and Formentera as San Fernando, for example, has become Sant Ferran and San Antonio, Sant Antoni. If you can read French and Spanish, the language is not too hard to figure out on paper but pronouncing it is another matter. Your efforts will, however, be appreciated.

Good Reading

Few books have been written about the Balearics but there are some great classics which give a fascinating insight into Spain generally.
• Hemingway, Ernest *Death in the Afternoon*. Hemingway's account of bullfighting, written during his sojourn in Spain in the 1930s.
• Hemingway, Ernest *For Whom the Bell Tolls*. Love story set in war-torn Andalucia.
• Hooper, John *Spaniards: A Portrait of the New Spain*. Sharp insight into the Spanish character.
• Lee, Laurie *As I Walked out One Midsummer Morning*. Romantic account of a young man's walk through Spain, pre-civil war.
• Morris, Jan *Spain*. Account of life in Spain in the 1960s.
• Richardson, Paul *Not Part of the Package*. (Pan). Modern history of Ibiza.
• Thomas, Hugh *The Spanish Civil War*. Definitive account of the civil war.
• Warner, Alan *Morvern Callar*. Disturbing modern fiction telling the story of a tourist blowing the savings of her dead boyfriend on the rave scene of the Spanish Costas.

INDEX

Note: Numbers in **bold** indicate photographs